Marriage

Over the Phone, Under the Radar and Behind the Badge

a collection of short stories from the ladies of CWHQ

ISBN: 1548091200
ISBN-13: 978-1548091200

Dedication

This book is dedicated to all law enforcement wives who have loved and lost. It takes a special woman to dedicate her life to support, love and care for a husband who has chosen law enforcement as his career. It takes a strong woman to walk beside him in all that he does and to support and protect the thin blue line. May God protect our families, both blood and blue.

We also dedicate this book to the men and women who have paid the ultimate sacrifice. Members of our group include:

Wayne Shirley	EOW: April 28, 1982
Brian Nichols	EOW: February 17, 2002
Travis Murphy	EOW: May 26, 2010
Victor Decker	EOW: October 26, 2010
Gale Stauffer	EOW: December 23, 2013
Brian Jones	EOW: May 30, 2014
Johnnie Jones	EOW: October 20, 2014
Christopher Kelley	EOW: June 24, 2015
Chad Dermyer	EOW: March 31, 2016
Dustin James	EOW: April 18, 2017

Acknowledgments

We would like to thank Jess Morris for designing, creating and illustrating the cover of this book.

We would like to thank all the women in our group that shared their personal stories of sacrifice and challenges that they have experienced within the Thin Blue Line family. Each name will be with their personal story.

We would like to thank Deirdrah Racine for providing the title of the book.

We would like to thank the admins of CWHQ for all their hard work in keeping an amazing group of women together and for their support.

The Thin Blue Line is not only the officers, but includes their spouses, which are instrumental in keeping the Thin Blue Line strong.

Note

To protect the anonymity of our members, their stories will be shown in Italics throughout the book. There are some that have given permission to state their name and others who have not. Please respect the privacy of these members.

Contents

Introduction

Today, thanks to social media, everyone feels that they know and understand the lives of those around them. Let's be honest, often, you are just seeing the "best" side of them and their family, and only what they allow you a glimpse of. So many couples have this "perfect love" persona if you will and you think you know them, you think you understand the tiny hardships they work through (such as who used the last bit of coffee up, he forgot to take out the trash again, she didn't pick up his dry cleaning, etc.) Even after their ten minute live Facebook rant, they will jump back onto their profile and post a picture of them kissing or something equivalent, to show the strength and perfection of their relationship. However, that is not real life.

Doing life with someone else is hard, marriage is not all sunshine and rainbows. You must be committed to that person, not only on their good days, but on their rough ones as well, when all of their flaws are showing like a neon light. Real commitment is forged during all the most ordinary of moments. Understanding sacrifices that are required in any marriage, are even more so in the marriage with your hero. You aren't just marrying the man. You are marrying the badge and his job. While that may sound cliché, it is absolutely true. These heroes can't just turn off the job. Their training doesn't allow it. They will forever be scanning the crowd not wanting to sit where they can't face the door, they are always on. It is heavy for them but it will also leave its mark on you as well. You can't love someone with the badge and not have it also change you.

A police officer is always on duty. He is willing to continually lay his life on the life for the rest of his blue family but also do the same for anyone in his community, no questions asked. He is brave, noble, strong, reliable. He faces danger without hesitation when the rest of us would want to run away. We are so blessed by the police officers that are in all our communities and we wouldn't make it without them. However, with their job, what they must deal with during shift and afterwards, how they often they must decompress after the bad calls, not any woman can handle.

It takes a special person to stand next to their hero, to support him on the good days and the bad. You must be willing to not only take on the challenges of marriage in general, but marriage to a cop. You must be willing to fight harder for him and for your marriage. They deal with the worst of the worst day in and day out and you are their support system. Police wives are in a category all to themselves.

Police wives are strong, selfless, brave, tenacious, and independent. That last one, being independent, is what breaks a lot of women from liking the uniform to being all in, being in love with the hero, not in love with a fantasy. This life means we, as the wives, must handle so much on our own. There are family cookouts, holidays, kids' football games or recitals, that you must go to on your own because he will be working. He will be serving the community that he loves and you will learn how to make random days special. It will no longer be about the date on the calendar, but whatever day he has off and you are able to make just as special. You will have to pull things together at home, handle things that otherwise you might not have to. You will also learn that every bit of it, every sacrifice, each thing you have to put more effort into is absolutely and most definitely worth it.

You see the love and passion that he has for his job and you wouldn't change that for the world, even if it meant he was home every night and on time, for dinner. Those little things that would make so many women walk away, are the things that we get to do for our heroes. It's not a chore to be their partner in every sense of the word. Partners cover for each other, they have each other's back no matter what.

One of the hardest things about being a police wife is having to share the love of your life with all the darkness that they face when they leave home to go serve another shift. You watch them get their uniform on, begin to strap on the velcro on their vest, and your heart starts to sink a little and races all at the same time. You know that you must keep your game face on, help him get his things together (making sure he actually has it all because we all know how often we have had to run out at midnight because they left something), kiss him and tell him how much you love him. Then you watch as your heart goes out the door with him. You won't get it back until he comes safely home and you hear the rip of the velcro and know that he is safe and sound for another night.

Being a police wife is the best worst life you could ever ask for! There are days that will make you wonder if you are the only one that has felt that way, been frustrated over that, or wishing you had someone else that understood what your life was like as a cop's wife. Here is your answer, this book. This book has been an absolute labor of love to reach out to other police wives and help you to realize that we do get it. We understand the cold dinners, not getting a call or text for hours, continually showing up to events by yourself and getting asked if he does actually exist. Hopefully, this book will give you a little comfort, knowing that you are walking this road with so many amazing police wives. We all know that people talk about the brotherhood etc., but what people do not realize is that the sisterhood of police wives is even better and stronger than that. We have each other's back no matter what, and we will always understand what you are going through! So, curl up in your favorite spot with a blanket and drink and jump into this adventure that we all love with our whole hearts.

1 Before the Blue

I never had any interest in dating a cop, let alone marrying one. When I was in high school, a couple of my friends had fathers in law enforcement. I noticed that their fathers were not home a lot. I noticed that their mothers were often stressed. They didn't seem too pleased with their father's career. While I respected law enforcement very much, I didn't want the home life that I noticed in my friends' homes.

Years later a good friend of mine set me up with a friend of hers. He hadn't been a police officer long, but he was still a police officer, and I wasn't so sure about it. I agreed to go because, I mean come on, it was hot that he was a cop even if I had no desire to date one seriously. My plan was to go on a few dates, have a few laughs, get it out of my system, and move on. A few harmless dates wouldn't hurt anyone, right?

What I didn't count on was how wonderful he would be. Our first date was a dream. He was handsome, confident, funny, an intelligent conversationalist, and a perfect gentleman. Looking back on it, I am pretty sure I was a goner from that first date on. Our second date *was fabulous as well, and the third, and the fourth. In between the dates we had fantastic phone conversations.*

One night he called me from work on his cell phone. He lost reception and the call dropped. I started picturing all sorts of horrible scenarios. I thought "what if he has been shot" and I started thinking about driving into the city to find him. I was irrational, and paranoid, and that was when it hit me that I was not just dating him for fun anymore, I must really love him. I had meant to break it off before it got serious, but it was all so amazing that I made excuse after excuse to put off breaking up. Next thing I know, I'm the fool getting in the car to go find my officer when he called back to apologize about his phone dropping the call. My reaction scared me enough to set aside time to talk to him the next opportunity he had.

I explained to him that I had no desire to be serious with an officer and why I had no desire to be seriously involved with an officer. He listened with a lot more understanding than I had anticipated. His father was a cop too, so he understood. He told me that it did not have to be that way. That those are the officers that live their job instead of understanding it is just a job. He said if both of us only treat it as a job and not a lifestyle that it doesn't have to be a lifestyle. This meant not bringing friends home from work or making friends with their wives or girlfriends. It meant not talking about it when he wasn't working. It meant "not bringing the job home" in his words which meant ignore it completely. It seemed so simple. Of course, if we don't treat it as a lifestyle it doesn't have to be one, right? Wrong.

We moved in together and I started to notice things that were off. He sweated at night, every night. If I startled him, his response was more aggressive than other people. We would be watching TV and get into arguments because he would just turn the channel without warning in the middle of a show. I noticed that he was super tense now when we went out, to the point that it was unnerving to be in the car with him just because of the tension rolling off his body. In restaurants he wasn't focused on me anymore, he was always scanning the place. Eventually we stopped going out entirely. Eventually we stopped watching TV together. Eventually I started avoiding him.

I came across a book for police wives. Even though I just knew it wasn't his job because he said it wouldn't be if we only treated it as his job, which we had done. However, at this point we were living like roommates so I figured it couldn't hurt to read the book. That book was just what I needed to bring back hope into my relationship. I recognized so much of my officer in that book. Understanding that his behavior wasn't personally directed at me was pivotal. Up until I had read the book I had been thinking, "he must be annoyed by me. I'm not what he wants but he doesn't have the courage to break up with me." Because that was how it felt. Understanding that it wasn't personal, helped me want to fight for the relationship to be healthy again.

I read a couple more books on the subject and joined some online groups for cop wives. Through talking to other cop wives, I heard so many similar stories. Their struggles were the same as mine. They understood completely and I felt less alone, and less judged. This gave me the confidence to ask for advice. It also provided people in my life who knew enough about what it was like to give good advice. I noticed the more I adjusted my life to be a cop wife life the better things were getting at home. I know my husband meant well when he said to not treat is as a lifestyle, but you must treat it as a lifestyle.

This job is not just a job, no matter how vigilantly you treat it as such. They cannot hang it up with their uniform at the end of the day and leave all the emotion in their locker (no matter how much they wish they could). If they don't find an outlet for it, it will come out in other less desirable ways. They will miss holidays, birthdays, sporting events, and anniversaries. Understanding that you signed on for a lifestyle and not just his job will help you be more understanding when you have to have Christmas on the 27th of December, or spend Valentine 's Day alone with a wine bottle and Netflix. Understanding that he isn't ignoring you when he scans a restaurant, and he isn't regretting being out with you when he tenses up for seemingly no reason, will keep you two from having many unnecessary arguments and hurt feelings. Understanding the global effect it has on all your lives will help you to recognize and head off problems before they become problems. Read books about it, join a support group, at least make friends with other wives.

My husband was correct in saying that it doesn't have to be stressful and awful, he was just wrong about how to keep it from being that way. With the right understanding, the right communication, and the right support group I think a police marriage can be so much stronger than the typical marriage. It only becomes

*stronger because the lifestyle forces you to truly understand each other. It only becomes stronger because the lifestyle forces you to develop confidence in your own abilities individually and together. It only becomes stronger when you admit and embrace the fact that it is a lifestyle and not just a job. I mean, after all, the reason you fell in love with him in the first place probably had something to do with him living the ideals of his job (justice, protecting the weak, doing the right thing always), not just working his job. Right? Right!
~Deirdrah*

Life before our heroes was quite different than the lives we are living now! Before the blue, your entire outlook on life is different. Nothing has come in and shaken up how you lived. We were going to and from work and not stressing and worrying about anyone's safety. We would go into restaurants and sit wherever we felt like sitting, we didn't know that people actually stress about their seat and make certain that they are always facing the door. We could go home, watch tv, hang with friends, and then when we went to bed, we were able to fall asleep right away and not wake up in the middle of the night worrying about anyone. Life was simple, normal, ordinary. We didn't realize what we were getting into when we met our hero.

We had been talking for several weeks by phone, text, and email, before we ever met in person. We wanted to really get to know each other, really talk about things, about what we enjoyed, what we wanted out of life, what we wanted in a relationship. We covered pretty much every topic under the sun. We got into a fight the weekend we were supposed to finally meet and he turned around and went home (he was in TN, I was in SC). By that point, honestly, I was already pretty much a goner for him. The weeks of talking about everything and looking forward to the next text or phone call, I was not about to let a stupid fight ruin everything. (He was more than a little stubborn about ever admitting that he could possibly be wrong or apologize).

So, I drove up to TN. I stayed with family that first night and texted him to let him know I was up and I still wanted to see him. He was not as convinced. However, that night a massive tornado tore through his town. He was working and trying to deal with the damage and the people that had been hurt. I really hadn't decided what I was going to do the next morning because it is not in me to just give up on something, but I didn't want to make things worse. So, I went to sleep that night hoping I would have an idea that morning.

Well, he ended up having the idea. He was exhausted from working the tornado damage, but sent me a text that if I wanted to come over I could and we could talk. He told me that he was tired and would still be in uniform, but told me where to meet him, then I just followed him back to his place. I was so nervous. I hate confrontation first of all, so I hated that a fight had happened anyway. I just wanted to make things right. So, we got to his place and I was freaking out on the inside, but kept a calm face on, mercy that was hard! As I walked up and he got out of his car, that was it. I was head over heels for him, I knew that was it. I had fallen in love with him through our conversations for several weeks, the texts, emails, calls, etc., but being there with him, and he was exhausted, I could see it all over his face, but oh my sakes he looked so sexy in that uniform. That did it! So not only was I into him for him, how he looked in the uniform was straight up the fabulous icing on the cake!

He showered and changed, and I was still nervous as all get out! Holy Smokes! He finished up and then we talked. Just like we had on the phone. We talked through the argument and then talked about everything else under the sun. The time flew by. I knew I needed to head home because it was a six hour drive and I had to work the next day, plus he had to work again that night so he really needed to get some sleep beforehand! It was so hard to say goodbye to him that day. I had missed him before, in between calls and emails etc., but after getting to be with him, it was so much worse.

Because our schedules were completely opposite, we had to figure out how we were going to make the long-distance deal work, because we were determined to make it work. So, I started leaving work on Friday, and driving up to his place. We would hang out for a couple hours, then when he had to go into work, one of his supervisors allowed me to do ride alongs with him while he worked. So that was our "date" night when I would be up for the weekend. I would get several hours in the car with him, plus getting to see what he actually had to deal with on a nightly basis. It gave me a very real look into the life that I was signing up for and I loved it. I loved seeing him work, I was so proud of him and what he had chosen for a career. Plus, riding along with him gave us hours to talk, about everything. And it made me love him even more. The long-distance deal was not fun, but we made the best of it for about four *months.*

We got engaged about a month in and planned a September wedding. I was going to move, leave my family and friends and start my life completely over in Tennessee. While that may have been scary for some, I was beyond excited. I loved Tennessee and while I did hate to leave my family, I was ready to be with him, and start our life together. I was fully committed to him and to what my life would become as a cop's wife.

Let me encourage you to make time to talk, really talk to each other. It may come and happen easily at the beginning, but life gets busy, schedules get hectic, and the longer they are on the job, the more cynical, the more negative, short tempered, and withdrawn they can get at times. Be willing to fight for each other, fight for your marriage. It is always worth it to fight and find a way to make it work. Sometimes you just need to remember why you got together in the first place. Remind him why he fell for you in the first place, tell him he needs to remind you why you fell for him. Sometimes you just need that crash cart for your relationship, shock it back into rhythm and make the changes you need to.

Always let him know how much you love him, how proud you are of him, and that regardless of what happens, how he acts, if he gets off track, you are there for him. Show him that you still love him and will still work on each other, that you will fight to make it better, to make it work. Sometimes it just may take a 2X4 to make them wake up and realize what is on the line, and what they need to snap out of it.

You chose him. You love him with all your heart. This life isn't easy, and you have to survive a lot of changes,

*but every single one is worth it. It is always worth the
work, hassle, and sacrifice. So, let him know that
today! Let him know that you still choose him, over and
over, day after day. Because that is exactly how I have
always felt! -Jess*

Maybe you are newly married and more than a little
overwhelmed with all of this, I promise this book, full
of blunt honesty about this life, is going to help.
Perhaps you have been married for a while and things
just aren't like they used to be and you are at your
wits end, you just don't know what to do about it.
Again, you will love this book and I hope it shows you
that it is worth it to fight for your marriage. Make
things right, put in the work. You might be a seasoned
cop wife and you have been through the ups and
downs, a few times, you will relate to most of this, too.

It really doesn't matter what you imagine this life
might be like when you first go out on a date with your
officer, you end up being wrong about a lot, if not all of
it. Hollywood and Network Television do not paint an
accurate picture (as we have all heard from our
husbands), and often we are shooting blind as we
begin walking this road.

We picture the strong, handsome, chivalrous hero
who is going to be our best friend, who we will go on
adventures with and always feel safe with, and that is
all good and usually true. We forget to include the
harder aspects of this life: feeling like you play second
to the job, the hectic schedules, last minute
cancellation of plans, his high stress level that can
come out in less than favorable ways.

At the beginning, we write everything off as minor, not a big deal, it won't happen again, usually it's not like this. Later nights than expected, them having to sleep most of the time that they actually are home, them getting upset over something that usually would be normal. We are still in the honeymoon phase and while we may not have stars in our eyes, we still aim to go over and beyond to make things easier on them, to be overly helpful, try and think of little things to make them smile while on shift. Sometimes, we second guess ourselves, wondering what did we really get ourselves into. Is it supposed to be this hard? Does anyone else ever feel like this or our we officially the absolute worst wife in the world?

On a sunny September morning in 2002, I was running late for church. That was not out of the ordinary, but that week I was not leading worship so I quietly took my seat close to the back. As soon as I sat down, I glanced a couple rows up and saw a new guy sitting with the preacher's daughter. My heart leapt and I knew instantly that I needed to meet this mystery guy. Little did I know then he was only, but a very mature, almost seventeen-year-old. I had just turned twenty the week before. We talked and hung out all the time. J and I quickly fell in love and married in July 2004.

From the time we met, we talked about our future and what God had in store for us. J had mentioned a desire to be a police officer but I knew that life was not for me. I could not imagine the love of my life putting his life on the line every day and I made that very clear. For me, it was not even an option as a career choice. We both wanted a family and I could not get over the fear of losing him. J did warehouse work and decided to go back to school to become a teacher. We started our family in 2006 and like most other young families with *house and car payments, we struggled financially. In September of 2008 I was online paying our water bill and happened to look at the employment opportunities section. Our city was hiring police officers. The amount they paid was a lot in comparison to what he was making at the time. That weighed heavily into my decision to mention it to J. He was nonchalant about it, but I filled out the form to start the application process. He went to take the test in November of that year and at that point it became real. All the fears I had, rushed in and I was an emotional basket case. We quickly learned he placed 6th, not bad considering they gave extra points to military, something J did not get. At the time we had no idea how many they were hiring or if J was even qualified. By late December, after an oral board, physical and in-home visit we knew he was going to get offered the job. All that was left was the polygraph, which we had total confidence he would pass.*

On February 9, 2009, J officially started his career as a Police Officer. He worked in the property room while the department worked to hire a second person from the list. In March, J and the other recruit were sent to the police academy. I remember being so torn emotionally. I was so proud I could barely put into words my excitement on starting this new adventure with him, but at the exact same time I was terrified at what the streets had in store. J and I shared everything. It just came naturally since we basically "grew up" with each other. There is not a thing in our lives that we do not talk about and that was no different while he was in the academy. He would come home and talk about what they did, what he learned, and his feelings about all the above. There was one day he came home and shared some books I should go get and read to prepare me for the "Police Wife Life". Of course, I ran right out and bought them. I think I made it through the first two chapters of one and was done with it. I am not a big reader anyway but the advice they were giving was, "don't ask a bunch of questions", "let him have down time" and it said there are things that he would not want to share with me. I knew our relationship better than any book did, so I decided ours was strong enough that I did not need a book to prepare me for my new life.

In August 2009, J graduated from the Police Academy. You could not wipe the smile off his face. For the first time I saw joy about where he was in his professional life. He was something...he was Police Officer. I was overwhelmed with pride. My husband, yes mine, was now a police officer! Wow, I could not believe how far we had come in the seven years since we met. A couple months after his graduation I became pregnant with our second child. He was completing his field training and we were living a picture-perfect life.

In June 2010 we were blessed with our second child, a daughter. Our first born, a son, was laid back, never cried and was a big bundle of love. That was not the case however with our beloved daughter. Our princess was definitely high maintenance. While I was a stay at home mom, and helping take care of my sick dad during the day, J was finding his place on patrol and was excelling. Even bringing home Rookie of the Year. Our picture-perfect life started to become a little tenser though.

J worked night shift, six in the evening to six in the morning. We stopped going to church because we always had an excuse, either he was working or sleeping and getting two kids ready was just a lot. I

noticed J was becoming short tempered, a far cry from
the man I had always known. I watched him as he
started interacting with us like we were suspects on the
streets. His demeanor, hand motions, stance, were all
indicative of a police officer talking to us, not my
husband or my kids' father. Being sleep deprived and
overwhelmed with his schedule, a newborn, 3-year-old
and every day chores and life, I convinced J to change
shifts and work days. That is when life (temporarily) fell
apart.

They bid for shifts every six months so January
2011, J started on days. Day shifters at our department
are full of people who have put in their time and are just
there for a paycheck, total opposite of J who truly loves
his job and desires to go above and beyond all the time.
He hated every single second of it, and made it known
to me every single day. He was there late almost every
day because the rest of his shift stopped answering
calls at five to ensure they got off at six on the dot. The
happy life of him being home at night for dinner and to
put the kids to bed quickly diminished. He worked more
hours of overtime and extra jobs than I ever knew was
possible for one man. He was providing for us like he
never had before, but it was at the expense of time with
us. The animosity for his shift continued to grow daily.

One call in particular sent him over the edge. On this
call there was an intoxicated, out of control person. J
got there and there was supposed to be a backup in
route. His backup was a fifty something female, Officer
H. J is on a street that the one and only officer who has
ever been killed in our city was on when he was shot.
There is not an officer in the city that should not know

where this street is. She apparently did not. While trying to wait for backup, things escalate and J must go "hands on" with the suspect because his Taser malfunctioned. J is telling units to "step it up" which means run code. He can hear sirens but they just are not getting to him. When Officer H finally shows up J is on the ground with the suspect and is yelling "taze him! Tase him." Officer H however, just stands there. She did not deploy the Taser until the guy gets up at which point he runs on top of Officer H's car. J grabs his baton and the guy flies off the car at him knocking the baton out of his hand and all the while she is just standing there. J did not feel like lethal force was ok in this situation and that is all he had left. Other back up arrived, they subdued the suspect, and he was taken into custody and transported to jail. This incident not only validated every fear J had about the day shifters, but also left me at fault for convincing him to make the move from the safety of night shift.

In late April, early in the morning, I get a call from J asking when the last time I had seen one of our friends, Case, post on Facebook. He had seen a call on the screen to locate Case's parents for a death notification. We found out that he had died in a car accident. Case's family owns the towing company most police departments in our area contract with. It was a given that we would attend his funeral. I did not, however, realize the deep emotional impact it was going to have on me. As we caught up to join the line of police cars and tow trucks heading the forty miles west for the funeral, it hit me. Hard. I had not been to a funeral since J became a police officer. I had watched clips of them on the news and cried right along with families, and watched hundreds of officers come from all over the country to honor the fallen officer. As we made our way to the exit and I could see the dozens of tow trucks and several dozen officers from cities all over north Texas and I realized this is in a way, what it would be like at a police funeral. I could not gather myself the rest of the day. I watched the church fill, the slides of his kids, family and friends and all I could think was this could be my husband. I could be living this one day. I could be the one comforting my kids even though I have no idea how I am going to even get up from the seat much less pick up the pieces of my life. The job J does and the risks he takes became crystal clear that morning. That next week we sat down with our friends and planned two vacations. We were going to live life.

In May of that year however, J and I almost called it quits. We had bought an above ground pool, and he asked his best friend CP, a sergeant with the same department, to come help him. Being on an emotional rollercoaster from the stresses of J's job, having a sick dad I was helping take care of during the day, two kids, a friend that just died, our former best friends that we had spent every day with for years decided to get a divorce and about to get a visit from Aunt Flo, it upset me that he didn't ask me to help. All I wanted was to be included. I did not and do not like to depend on anyone to help us with anything. I honestly do not remember all the details of what sparked that fight.

I remember that he was getting ready for another off-duty job and that CP was going to swing by and get him since he was working it as well. He was in uniform by the time it escalated to yelling. He pushed me onto *the couch and I got up and hit him in the face. That was something I had never done so it surprised us both. It was not hard but enough to upset him even more. I did my typical and told him to just leave if he did not want to be here and married to me only this time he seemed ready to have a break. I was making my way out of the kitchen trying to get to the bedroom to pack his stuff for him. Ok, I was going to throw it outside, but you get the point. I went to move past him and he was blocking me. As I put my arm up to push him out of the way he had keys in his hand and cut my arm. It was a pretty good gash and about seven inches long. I remember not looking at it because I did not want to give him the satisfaction of knowing he hurt me. A few minutes later CP arrives, in uniform, and in total shock at what he is witnessing. This was not the norm for us. We were always a happy couple, laughing and holding hands. CP is looking at my arm and looking at me. He then asks "What happened? Was it mutual?" I knew I had a choice. Even in my anger and hysteria I knew. Friend or not he would take J to jail if he had assaulted me. I immediately told him it was mutual. He asked again and I reiterated I was fine while J was packing up some of his belongings. He left that night without his phone, with all his important belongings and our Tahoe. Since I was a stay at home mom we only had one vehicle so him leaving in it left me with two kids and no transportation. Not long after him and CP left, CP's wife and another police wife showed up to get the story. We are close with them and had planned two vacations with them in the coming months so this was not unexpected.*

*After crying all night and all day the next day I
literally could not cry any more tears. I was exhausted
and trying to explain to my son and daughter why
daddy was not home. I have never been so heart
broken. J had never treated me the way he did that
night and been so callous about it. I knew the job had
changed him. It hardened him. He was quick tempered
and didn't want to put up with my emotions any more.
The stresses of police life, shift work and everyday life
caught up with him. I pled with him to come home and
talk it out. He insisted on CP being present, which tore
me up inside. He said he thought I was going to try and
cost him his job and he wanted a witness. It was like I
was speaking to a totally different person. The man I
loved and had known for eight years by then seemed to
be gone. I was devastated. My whole world was turning
upside down because we both let our emotions get the
best of us.*

*Once we could talk openly and honestly, barriers
we did not even realize existed, the ones that began
building up after he started at the police department,
started to crumble. We went to counseling and got back
into church. We decided that every day we were going
to choose us and work on our marriage and family.
Marriage is like weight. Just because you reach your
goal weight doesn't mean you stop working. You must
choose every day to make healthy decisions and work
out. Just like you work every day on your marriage.
Never stop learning new things and ways to improve
your relationship. We both started putting God first
again, ourselves second and our kids third. Everything
else was minor. We go to marriage seminars, classes at*

church, read books and have done devotionals together. Because we had lost our ability to effectively communicate we almost lost our marriage. We overcame. This year we celebrate our eleventh wedding anniversary. We are the proud parents of three beautiful kids and love each other more deeply than we ever could have dreamt about when we first got married. ~Indestructible~
~Amy Michlitsch

Over and over it is reiterated that we can all relate to the up and downs of our marriages with this life. Time and schedules crowd out any time for us as a couple, we quit making time to really talk to each other, and it tears up our marriages. That does not mean we give up on each other. You have to make it work, decide to start making time for each other again, go back to how everything started, how you fell in love to begin with, how and why you chose each other in the first place. This life is hard and challenging, but it works best as a team, when you have each other. So, fight for it. It is worth it. You connected unlike you had with anyone else so don't let that go.

It is always easier to leave, to stop trying, to give up and walk away. While we could never make a blanket statement, one size fits all, however, if like the story above with limited time together as a couple, not making a priority of really talking to each other, the stresses of the job, is the reason that the two of you have grown apart. Maybe this is what you needed to hear, to know that others have made it to the other side of this, past this life feeling more than a little overwhelming. We all came into this clueless as to what we were getting ourselves into, but we said yes for the best reason, we didn't want to do life without them. It's never too late to make things better again.

My husband likes to tell the story of how he wouldn't be a cop at all if it hadn't been for me. In fact, he would have gone to jail instead.

When we were in our early twenties, we loved to club. I'm not talking about ecstasy fueled raves or anything. In our smaller town we had two dance clubs within walking distance to each other. One of which he happened to be a DJ at. Boy were those fun days!

One not-so-fun night, a huge fight broke out in the club. I was knocked backwards and hit my head on the bar. I was trapped under the bar between a tangle of barstools. I may have blacked out because I don't remember the police coming in and telling everyone to get outside.

What I do remember is sitting outside the club on the sidewalk with a patrol car parked in front of us, unattended, door wide open. We were waiting for a cab because we both had been drinking. Suddenly, my husband jumps up and says, "here's our ride!" As he dashed towards the patrol car.

His right foot was in the car, but before he could slide in behind the wheel, I found super-human strength (and some choice words) and yanked that darling husband of mine out of the car before anyone else saw what happened. ~Amy T.

Your story may have seemed so ordinarily perfect, or perhaps hysterical after the hangover was slept off, or something so insane you initially wondered if it had really happened. Each of us has our own unique way that we started out in the blue family and each story is special in its own way, because it was what brought the beauty and the badge together. He needed exactly the woman that you are to be his partner. He saw in you the woman he wanted for his forever, for his best friend, secret keeper, encourager, strength, lover, shoulder to cry on, to weather the ups and downs with him. This life has so many trials in it, don't second guess your worth and value because you are in one of the trenches right now and he isn't taking time to remind you how important you are to him. Sometimes they need a gentle reminder, and let's be honest, with these heroes of ours, sometimes they need way more than a gentle reminder, but don't give up on them, and don't let them give up on you.

2 The Academy

There are two ways to get initiated into this life. There are some of us that fell in love with our hero while he was wearing that heart stopping uniform, knowing (well, we thought we knew) what his life was going to entail. The rest of our blue sisters walked another path into this life. They were already in love with their hero but he did not have a gun and badge, yet. They were living what the general public knows as a normal life. They weren't waiting each night for the sound of velcro being ripped apart as he came through the door and took his bullet proof vest off. They were enjoying regular schedules, date nights that were postponed due to texts saying something like "Sorry, stuck on a case, won't make it", "late call, gonna be a long one, sorry babe", and many others. These women had to stand by their heroes as they started this life.

When my husband began the police academy we had been married for about seven months and had just added a new baby to our clan a month prior. The first day my husband started the academy, I had to take our two-year-old son to the hospital to have surgery to remove his adenoids and tonsils. As a parent it's a scary thought to put your toddler under anesthesia but it was even harder not having my spouse there as well. That was the official start of the blue life.

Before my husband began the academy, he worked as a corrections officer for four years. I learned how to get used to the switching shifts and missed holidays during his employment at the jail. Fortunately, when he began the academy his class was only a forty-five-minute drive from our house, so he did get to stay home except during the EVOC course when they went up to Forsyth, which was only for three days. Just because he was physically home every night does not mean he was able to be present every night with myself and the boys.

Since we lived a good distance from the training center he would have to wake up extra early to be there on time for PT each morning then the drive home took extra time due to people getting off work at the same time. By the time he would get home he was so exhausted and had to study, so it was hard for him to spend a lot of quality time with us as a family.

In my experience this was the hardest part for me. I believe part of that was the fact that I was still on maternity leave and was staying home with my two-year-old and one month old so I had no adult interaction all day until my husband came home. Then by the time he showered and ate dinner it was time for bed so he could get up and do it all over again, not much time for cuddling or talking together. I must say though all in all we didn't have a bad experience since he was home during the entire course and off every weekend. The academy is the start of a "new normal" and each wife's experience will be different. - Kailyn

Just as this life looks different for each of us, so does the experience that each wife had while her husband was in the academy. This life is full of constant changes, ups and downs, and plenty of curve balls that start as soon as we begin walking by their side. While some of the guys are not allowed to go home each night during the academy, others have more flexibility and can physically go home each night; however, most of those wives will agree they don't get much of their attention. So often as wives, it is easy to compare ourselves, our marriage, our circumstances, to others. However, we forget that you cannot judge a book by its cover. Rarely will someone else get raw and real about the hardships, frustrations, and difficulties of any given time period or situation. This book is meant to give you the down and dirty aspects of this life and it's not an easy one.

So, my husband went to the Dayton Academy here in Ohio. It's an academy that you have to wait years to get into and they pay you to attend. On average, everyone that made it into his class waited about 2-3 years to get in. As you can imagine, we were excited when he was finally accepted. The best part was that the academy hours were 8-5, Monday through Friday. I also worked 8-5, Monday through Friday. We were about to have dinner together every night and enjoy weekends together. Although, this didn't help me adjust to the thought and idea of becoming a police wife. A challenge for me, was watching my husband go through the academy and struggle with some of the testing, and having difficulty studying the Ohio revised code. They were required to write large portions of the revised code to pass.

On another note, there were only 12 people in his class. Four of these people were women. In the beginning, everything was fine, but as the academy went on and the 12 of them grew closer, the rumors began. There was a flirtatious girl who was rumored to cheat on her spouse, and that's enough to make your head spin. She was in a committed relationship and was still expressing interest in married men. As the academy went on, the 12 of them had to exercise, practice defensive tactics, and suffer the same pains together. The best way to get through it is to trust and communicate, always. I was lucky in the fact that I had been with my husband already for six years and had no reason not to trust him. Aside from the heavy testing and physical demanding side of the academy, it was nothing for me compared to what cop wife life entails. – K. Williamson

While we do all share so much common ground, and can relate to each other when we can't relate to anyone else, we are still going to have different highs and lows at different times. That is one thing that makes this sisterhood so very special. A few wives may have really struggled during the Academy, having their husbands gone so many days in a row, or just being otherwise engaged and exhausted at night if he did make it home while others could manage it well, without much added stress or difficulty.

When Jake and I first started dating we both worked for a rental company and saw each other every single day. After 2 months of dating he decided that he wanted to join the police academy. I felt all kinds of emotions. I was nervous, a little upset, and scared. I knew that Jake would make an excellent police officer but I also knew how officers were treated. My stepdad has been a police officer for over 20 years and I had heard plenty of stories that made me despise people. I didn't want to see Jake disrespected in the ways that I know some people disrespect cops. I told Jake that I supported his decision but I was very concerned about what it meant for us as a couple in a new relationship. Before he started the academy, Jake straight up told me that it would be hard. That we wouldn't get to see each other as often or talk all the time. As a 21-year-old girl I was crushed. I thought for sure that meant the end of our relationship. There were days where we only got to send a few texts. There were weeks where I only saw him once in the span of 7 days. But he was absolutely loving the academy. He was at the top of his class and so dedicated to what he was doing. We experienced all the major changes that come with being a cop together. He never once made me feel like I wasn't important to him because he had other things going on.

Lucky for us we only lived about 2 minutes away from each other, and tried to squeeze in as much time together as possible. Having a stepdad who is an officer was extremely helpful to me because I knew what to expect. I knew that Jake becoming a police officer meant that I would be spending holidays alone. That he would probably be working night shifts for a long time. I wasn't going into it completely unaware of what was going to change. I am still incredibly nervous every time I see him putting on his vest but here we are, 3 years later and I am married to a man who loves what he does and I couldn't be prouder of him. -Kayla

When my husband and I started dating we were only 23 years old and he was a corporal in the county jail. This position required the same shift work that the road deputies work: 12-hour shifts, one month of nights, one month of days and so on. So, I had become somewhat accustomed to that work schedule. Four months after we were married, at the age of 24, he told me he was being considered to go to the academy to become a road officer. I was very nervous about him going to the road, but I knew it was something he really wanted to do so, after hours of discussion, we decided if it were offered to him, he would do it. Not long after, he was headed to the academy – 4 months of regular 9-hour days!

I know most people wouldn't say they enjoyed their husband's time in the police academy but I really did. I was a graduate student at the time and doing a full-time internship in the same town where he was enrolled in classes. So, we could get lunch together at times and we were pretty much on the same schedule – something that has not happened since the academy. The only downfall for me was all the schoolwork that is completed at home, and the pressure to make sure he got through it successfully the first time. However, he is diligent and all worked out well. I think adjusting to him being on the road and going back to shift work was much more of an adjustment than having to adjust to him being in the police academy. -LM

All our heroes had to survive their time at the academy. Some departments allow just the academy that is run in multiple areas of the state to qualify for a position, while others require each candidate to go through their own academy, regardless of if that candidate has already survived a state one. Academies have differing lengths and specialized requirements, but the result is the same. If you survive through your time at the academy, you will be able to graduate and then begin work as a certified officer.

Graduation day is what both the heroes and their wives countdown to. The academy isn't just some school you have for a few months. The guys are away from home for months! Often, they are restricted on how often they are even allowed to call home. So, for several months, you don't get to talk to each other every day, and you definitely don't get to see them on a regular basis anymore. The best way to communicate is through letters back and forth. Letters are such a lost art of communication, we are all used to being able to pick up the phone and know exactly where someone is, being able to relay a story or something that just took place, immediately. Letters? Not the same. You must write out all of your thoughts, put it in an envelope, put a stamp on it, put it in the mail, and then wait several days for them to receive it. That works both ways with the Academy.

Not only are the wives having to wait several days for their letters to reach him, they are waiting to receive a letter from him as well. That letter means everything to them. That is the only way that they know he is ok. That is how they tell their husbands how much they love him, that they are waiting for him, and that they just can't wait until Graduation.

There are fewer things in life that have made me prouder than watching my husband walk across the stage to achieve his dream of becoming a police officer. I've had not only the pleasure of witnessing this once, but twice. The first time was in 2008. My husband graduated from PTI to become a city Police Officer in my hometown. The 14-week academy seemed long at the time, but wasn't too painful. It wasn't set up like military boot camp as they lived in apartments and got to call home every night. Although they had a curfew, nobody was breathing down their neck every minute of the day. He came home on the weekends and we worked on our first house we just bought. We didn't have any kids yet either as we had only been married a year at that point. It wasn't ideal being apart as somewhat newlyweds, but it went by smoothly, and I soon became an official cop wife.

Fast forward three and a half years to 2011 where we were a family of three plus two dogs. My husband loved his line of work, but started keeping his options open for bigger and better paying law enforcement opportunities. He soon got the chance of a lifetime to fulfill his true dream, to follow in the footsteps of his hero Grandpa, and become a State Trooper. With this step up in pay and benefits, I would also get to fulfill my dream to stay home with our daughter. Plus, we knew this would bring a location change for us, which was both exciting and scary. The only thing that stood in the way was a 26-week para-military academy. My husband rarely gets nervous, but the morning of check-in was by far the most anxious I have ever seen him. We knew this wasn't going to be easy, not only being apart, but starting all over again in a career he knows, and being treated like a nobody, too. Plus, in this academy, there would not be nightly phone calls to hear about each other's' day, his voice, or tell him about our 1-year old daughter's newest milestone. I was a wreck watching him drive away, but hopeful and confident in our future. On his first night, he got to make one phone call before putting his phone away for the week. I thought that call would give me peace for the week, but boy was I wrong. He said it was already terrible and he didn't know why he chose to do this again. He had no choice but to be tough and make it, but he was really questioning himself. It killed me to hear him so miserable. I worried about him all week as each day crept by. How were we going to make it through 26 weeks of this?

On the positive side, he came home every weekend and we cherished our family time together, but Sundays were the absolute worst. A lot of tears were shed, even from him, which is far from normal. We knew each week down, meant we were closer to getting through, but the days in between were so long. For one, the cadets got in trouble for everything from not making their beds correctly to messing up in Drill, to their bunks and uniforms not being neat enough. It seemed to be more about doing all that stuff perfectly than learning the actual job, so it was frustrating at times. For me, I was working part time a few afternoons a week while my mom watched our daughter. We didn't find out what district we were getting assigned to until almost halfway through the academy. Once districts were picked, I was in charge of getting our house ready to sell, dealing with the realtor, and looking for a place to live in our new area 3 hours away, all while caring for our 1 year old. Although not easy, those activities were good distractions to keep my mind and body busy, which helped pass the time quicker.

As I mentioned before, the cadets didn't get to call home nightly. In fact, they didn't earn their first call until week seven so what did we do to communicate? We wrote and mailed letters to each other. As hard as it was not getting to call, there were fewer more exciting things than walking back from the mailbox with a letter in hand ready to rip open. My husband always told me receiving a letter from me was the highlight of his week, other than getting to come home Friday evenings. It was so wonderful getting to read what was going on in not only my husband's day, but his thoughts and feelings as well. He is not one to talk about his feelings very much, so getting a glimpse into his heart and mind while away was so special. He opened up in a way that really touched my heart, and still does when I read them now.

You see, we were at a really good point in both our marriage and faith walk at the time the Academy started, and those relationships only grew throughout the process. I would send him little verses and thoughts from my daily devotions, as well as inspirational quotes and inside jokes. He would tell me what he'd been praying about and how much his faith was growing through the 6-month stint. I remember the movie "Courageous" came out while he was in the Academy. We went on an Anniversary date to see it while he was home. That movie really had an impact on him during that time, being a husband, Dad, and in the Police Academy. Even though we were physically apart so much, I never felt spiritually closer to him. Without prayer and our relationship with the Lord, the whole process would have been a lot tougher to go through.

We committed to being faithful and thankful to God for this blessing in our new life ahead. This was only the beginning! Although we already knew what the LE life was like with the fears, shift work, overtime, stigmas, etc., we were still starting a new journey in a completely new place. Other than the separate colleges we attended, we always lived near family and friends in our home area. Now, we were picking up and moving three hours away from everyone and everything we've ever known with our little girl. As nerve wracking as it was, we were excited and knew this was going to be really good for us, plus it wasn't too terribly far away. On top of that, our little family was going to be together again soon!

On February 9, 2012, the day before graduation, my daughter and I loaded up the last of our belongings that hadn't made the move to our new place yet. We then headed north to see our number one man. The academy held a Bell Ceremony that day and we got to see the facility where the training took place. That night, there was a banquet to celebrate the upcoming graduation. On Feb 10, we watched that man we love so much reach his dream. He not only graduated, but

*he got his star pinned on him by his hero, his Grandpa,
a retired State Trooper.*

*Three and a half years later, my husband is a well-
respected, hardworking Trooper, who has been
handpicked for many special details. We are now
transferred back to our home area living near family
again. On top of that, we have a little boy, now, too.
This life hasn't been easy. We've been through several
obstacles and hard times. Our faith has definitely been
tested. I've had many lonely, scary nights. I've
watched my man lose a friend in the line of duty, dealt
with him being talked to like garbage, and spent many
holidays and Anniversaries without him, amongst many
other things. One thing will always remain, though. I
will always support him, love him, be his biggest fan.
He's accomplished so much and I know will accomplish
more. I'll never forget where it all began, when we took
that leap of faith in starting over again to follow God's
plan for our family. I'll never forget the ups that we
celebrated, the downs that strengthened us, and those
precious letters. ~Lacey*

The academy is just the beginning of this life for
the officers, whether they already have us by their side
or not. They are pushed to their limits and beyond
during their weeks there. The officers are put through
intense training, for as many of the different areas and
scenarios that they will be facing as possible. They are
supposed to deal with a myriad of situations, people,
and outside forces and still be able to think on their
feet and make life and death decisions in mere
fractions of a second. But where does that leave the
wife?

We don't go through the academy. We don't get put
through training and instruction on how to handle
different situations that may occur with our husband,
or how to help him through scenarios he has to walk.
As wives we aren't given a how-to manual that will

help us navigate this life from the beginning. Chapter One, "Surviving Interrogation 101", how to survive a cop, a.k.a. your husband, interrogating you like a suspect without either being completely crushed or seeing red and being ready to commit a felony. Chapter Five, "The Art of Keeping Dinner Hot and Your Temper Cool", and so forth.

We are expected to somehow just know how to handle everything the right way, to not increase their stress level, or end up having their frustration taken out on us. Don't get me wrong, it's not always all their fault. Sometimes, we need to be better at simply reminding them that we are not fellow officers, we don't understand why they got so upset over something, or why they were adamant about something else and didn't allow any discussion. They stay in cop mode all the time because that is what their training has taught them, at times taking it out on us, the ones that are just trying to love and support them. I think that it is important for us to remember that. Instead of being hurt or angry over what they said or didn't say, or rather how they said it to us, a calm reminder that you are their safe place, no matter what, would go a long way. Sometimes these strong, brave men, just need us, as their wives, to remind them that its ok for them to be vulnerable with us.

So, does it make this life easier or harder to get used to, to get comfortable with, if you are with your husband when he first starts the life, being with him through the academy and training? We each have our own history of how we started out in this life, some before and some after the academy. Regardless how it started for each of us, none of us got our own handbook. Well, until this brilliant book, of course! So, while we can't make an absolute statement with any certainty of why one way is easier than the other, you can hear from several wives their thoughts on the matter!

-I think it would be harder if he became an officer after we met. When we started dating, he had already been a cop for a while. There was still an adjustment period for both of us (relationship wise) and we are still adjusting, but it's just how it's always been. We don't know how it would have been if he wasn't a cop, so we don't miss what we have never known. The only thing that has helped me with the transition has been to speak with other LEOWs.

-I think it would be harder to adjust if they became an officer after marriage. While dating, I got used to the schedule, but I would say that my life changed and became more negative for a while. I became more withdrawn and distrusting of people. I am not as outgoing as I used to be. I feel that connecting with other LEOWs and being a part of a group like CWHQ has been the most influential help. It's a safe place where we have all had similar experiences and are not alone.

-I've known him since high school, but he was a new rookie when we got married. I would think it would be easier to adjust to the lifestyle with him already being a cop. As a nurse I always worked shift work and holidays and things like that, so I totally understand and expected chaos ha-ha. It hasn't been until all the recent events and backlash that I've even noticed or felt any difference in before/after the Blue Life. We've always been cautious and vigilant, but still try to live life to the fullest and teach our children to do the same.

-When we met, J was an officer in the jail, and shortly after we got married he got sent to the academy and put on road patrol. The shifts were the same, but obviously the job description is vastly different. I think it would be harder to go from being with someone who has a normal job, you know, weekends off, holidays off and

works 8am-5pm, and then they become a cop. That would be a huge adjustment. I don't recall my anxiety being as high before I married into the blue family, but honestly, I contribute some of that to having kids also. I don't know that it can all be blamed on the blue life, but I spend more time alone, I am responsible for a ton around the house, and I don't sleep as well. Since all the anti-cop stuff the last few years, I also find myself feeling isolated and pissed off more often.

-While it is hard to say, I think it could be harder marrying someone who is already a cop because you're having to adjust to a life they already know, and that could potentially cause hardships, rather than learning the ropes together. However, both scenarios each bring different challenges.

-When J an I met, he hadn't even been through the academy yet. He became a police officer about a year after we had been dating, and I think it was easier on us because we were both kind of learning the lifestyle together, instead of him already being used to it.

3 About the Life

This life is not for the faint of heart. It is challenging, scary, heartbreaking, exciting, fantastic, allows immediate connection with other LEOWs, lonely, and so many other emotions, but hands down, most definitely and absolutely worth it. Every. Single. Time.

Unfortunately, we walk into this life blind. We truly do not have a good understanding of what the life, what their job, actually entails and how it really affects them; therefore, how it is going to affect us as their wife. They have to go through the academy and for several months they are taken through every scenario and trained what to do, what to expect, what to plan for with different calls, how to react to different situations and most importantly how to make sure that they make it home after their shift. But their training doesn't end there. After the academy, and they are hired on with a department, then they begin their Field Training with their FTO (Field Training Officer). This is their on the job training, with a seasoned officer to be there with them to help problem solve different situations, and ensure that they are ready to be out on their own. These officers have months of training and work in order to prepare them for this life and what do we as their wives get? Not much of anything! We simply try to understand as much as we can about why they have mood swings, or some days they don't want to talk about anything regarding work, and others they need to talk about it all.

We have to learn as we go, trying to still hit a homerun when a curve ball comes our way, but often failing. When we don't respond how they want us to, it can cause frustration for them and feelings of being a failure, not measuring up to what he needs, confusion over why he got upset at you, and more for us. This life is hard. These heroes encounter the worst of the worst during their shifts, and while many do try their best to shed themselves of the darkness from their job as they take off that uniform, oftentimes it is not that easy for them to do so. The spouses are left trying to juggle life at home and not knowing how to best support them. It is not just you that feels this way. All wives have felt confused, helpless, and hurt many, many times before. Honestly, that happens in every marriage but that happening when married to a police officer, those feelings are even more magnified. Sometimes not even your husband can control what may set him off, remind him of a bad call, the lack of sleep, nightmares, etc. What they are dealing with oftentimes comes out much more sporadically than what you would see with someone that has a different profession with minimal stress and risk. This is a lifelong process of learning each other, and learning the job. Because you are indeed married to him and to his job. It is a lot to handle and process at times. So, what are you supposed to do to make it easier?

There are several things that LEOWs would collectively agree can greatly improve your understanding of what they have to deal with on the job, as well as how to best help yourself be able to deal with the ups and downs that this life brings. One of the best ways to understand what they deal with, is to actually witness it firsthand! Many departments do allow spouses to do a ride along with their officer. This enables you to go with him to one of his shifts and ride around with him for several hours, or even his entire shift. You are able to witness every call that he receives, how he handles it, as well as see what he looks for, what grabs his attention as he drives around in his zone, making stops, etc. It also provides you with great one on one time with him. There is something about riding along with him that allows him to be the hero that you feel he is all the time, but so often he feels like he falls short of that. In that car, with his uniform on, he feels confident and sure of himself with you riding shotgun.

Allow him to be the hero to you. That seems like such a simple and obvious statement to all of us, because we saw him as our hero from day one. There really never was any other option, right?

Here's the thing, with time, two different scenarios can happen. Scenario one is that we just forget to tell him like we used to. We get into the routine called life, always crossing things off of our to-do lists, talking to and seeing each other but with less frequency as before. We are still head over heels for him and don't think that there is anyone in the world who can do it for us like he can but we stopped telling him that. As big and tough as our men may be, they still need to hear from us that they still fit the bill as our hero. That we respect him and adore him and that we still choose him each and every day. The second scenario may be harder to admit because maybe you haven't felt like he has been much of a hero to you lately. The long shifts, extra duty, not to mention the time he has to sleep when he's home, has left you feeling like you are there to cook, clean, have his uniform ready to go, and maybe once in a blue moon have sex with. You haven't been feeling like you make it on his to-do list, much less feel like any of his priorities. You haven't felt cherished, loved, or prioritized in you can't remember how long. He still wants to be your hero, but a lot of life and stress and shifted priorities have gotten in the way, on both sides.

It would be a lot easier if we could blame it all on them, what they have to deal with, and how it changes them. We can't. See, sometimes we as cop wives get just as good at avoiding the issues and before you get ready to say that's absolutely not true, hear me out. In the beginning, we do a lot of watching and waiting with them to see if they are going to need to talk something out, or if it's something they will choose to keep to themselves. We are trying to feel our way through the beginning. If we aren't careful, that can turn into a habit, become our auto-pilot mode, and that is where it gets dangerous and begins to cause problems. We have to always be partners, first and foremost, and if we choose to stop counteracting their silence and them coming home too many days in a row being standoffish, we are both going to suffer because of it. Then it gets easier to just not deal with it, and he starts to seem less like a hero to you and you aren't his safe place anymore. If that is where you are right now, it's ok. You can come back from that and then some! You just have to be willing to fight, fight for him, fight for you, fight for your marriage.

Ride along? An absolute perfect way to break that ice. Ask him about it and don't let up. It allows him to show you, up close, part of his world that affects every aspect of who he is. For wives that may have departments that do not allow you to ride with your husband, it can still be a great thing to do with one of his fellow officers, although you may not want a whole shift with someone else. Even riding along with someone else is going to give you fresh eyes for what he is dealing with every shift. It gives you some great conversation starters about his world and still lets him know how thankful you are for him and for what he does! Police officers are not able to simply turn that switch off when they aren't on duty. They are always on no matter where they are. As wives we have to understand that and learn how to accommodate that. It is a process, a learning experience that takes time, a lot of time, to really get a grasp on what he has to face every time he puts that vest and uniform on.

One of my most memorable ride alongs had to do with a DUI suspect. He was on midnight shift patrol and it just so happened to be the night after the huge Crawfish Festival that day. Let me preface all of this by sharing just how bad of a gag reflex he has. I have always been on-duty when the kids get the stomach bug, and this ride along should have been my warning sign that he wouldn't be helping to clean up puke after kids.

It had already been a pretty busy night, he was usually placed in one of the crazier and busier zones because he could handle it. We end up behind this small pickup truck. It was swerving all over the road so we start to follow. Next thing we see, is the passenger hang her head out the window and begin hurling all down the side of the truck. Disgusting, right?

So he lights them, calls it in, and pulls them over. This was going to be a no-brainer. So he gets out of the car and proceeds to walk up to the driver. He begins talking and initially it looked to me like a typical stop. He was behaving like he did with all suspects. Then I saw it. It must have finally registered for him what he was actually standing next to, what was inside of the truck. I see him distance himself and I can see him fighting his gag reflex. Not once, not twice, but multiple times. I was rolling! I knew that whatever he was seeing must have been bad. He had stepped further back from the driver's window to finish talking to him before coming back to the car.

When he got back inside the car, his gag reflex was still going, which of course, I thought was hilarious. He then informs me just what he had seen inside the truck. Telling me that we may have thought her puking out the window was bad, but it wasn't. She had already filled the truck up and he had been able to make out the crawfish in her vomit. Oh my goodness, I still laugh about that stop! He was not as amused and wanted to bathe in disinfectant and wipe his mind of that imprinted image. But oh the things we see and hear about in this life y'all! -Jess

Besides ride alongs, what else can you do to help you process this life better? Find a strong support group. There is nothing, absolutely nothing, as important as you having a strong and close knit support system that can walk this life with you. A support group gives you someone (or a lot of someone's) to text, call, or Facebook message at 2am when you heard from him three hours ago that this was a bad call and he needs you to know he loves you. As hard as you are trying to stay calm and know he is going to be just fine, you can't sleep, for as soon as you try to close your eyes the worst scenario flashes before you. You need those people that you can reach in the middle of the night and tell them what is going on and simply ask them to pray with you, to hear someone else say that he is going to be ok. That he will text again as soon as he is able. People who will keep checking back with you at 2:30am, 3:15am, until you do get that text or call saying it's over and he is ok. Sometimes, no matter how many times you have been through that exact same scenario while he is on duty, it never really gets any easier; however you know that he will call or text as soon as he is able to! You will continue to worry until he has checked back in with you and confirmed it. These days, not knowing how he is while he's at work, is so much harder than it ever was before. You need supportive friends that are in this life too, that truly understand everything you are dealing with.

You do not have to find it within the department that your husband works for, you may feel more comfortable connecting with other LEOWs that are spread out in other departments that may not be connected to your husband or his department at all, but you will still be able to come together like sisters. Let me encourage you to have at least one or two ladies that you can always go to about things you are dealing with in your marriage and with your husband. It is not wise to make your family your go-to for venting, especially in this life. It can be hard for us to handle and understand all the time and we are living it. Think about that in regards to your family, no matter how close you are with them, or how understanding they may be. Family will always tend to side with their blood. Our marriages are hard enough without adding in family pressures and drama, even if it's unintentional. You can and will forgive your husband, even on his worst days where he makes you beyond angry. It's a lot harder for a mom, dad, or sister to do the same thing after learning the ins and outs of your latest arguments, and yet 24 hours later you and him are great again.

While this life is amazing, hard, challenging, exciting, frustrating, and everything in between, it is what you decide to make it. We have the power to make it easier or harder on ourselves and our spouse. We can either use every unexpected thing from his job to get angry over, build resentment, and cause more fights and frustrations, or we can truly understand and accept what we signed up for. We need to allow ourselves the range of emotions but make a commitment to always let the petty stuff go. We need to ensure that we are his safe place, to be his support system and partner. Understanding that they already have so much on their plate, why in the world should we add more stress to it?

When I met my husband, he was already a police officer, a game warden if we are being technical. I could tell that he really loved his job and enjoyed being outdoors and working the hunting areas and waterways. I was a little shy about meeting him because of his profession and I wasn't sure how our first date was going to go. Obviously, it went well and a year and a half later we were married.

I remember when we were dating his job didn't bother me as much. Sure, we had to make some adjustments, but it wasn't a huge deal at the time. I remember it changing when we got married. The only reason I can think of is that with marriage came the realization and stresses of what his job actually entailed. When we got married, we were living in a big city that was close to his family but four hours away from my family. I hated it with a passion. I didn't know anyone outside of his family at the time and I grew up in a small town, so the big city life was definitely not for me. The traffic was the worst part. Of course, being in a big city, my husband was a lot busier than he had been when we started dating. I felt like most days he was home enough to eat, bathe, and sleep and that was it. So, about 6-8 months in to our marriage I really started to resent his job. I felt like I always had to do everything alone all the time! It was to the point that when I went to the grocery store I got jealous when I saw couples shopping together.

I felt like this for the first two years of our marriage. It caused added stress to our marriage and it caused unhappiness in our marriage. Then, something happened. It was a day that we were both at home, I was reading a book or something and my husband was watching tv and I remember looking over at him and he looked completely exhausted. It was like the light bulb went off in my head. I thought to myself, as I looked at him, that here is a man, my man, that gets up every day and goes and does a selfless job and puts up with all the crap all day long, and then here I am being selfish and wanting more time, more holidays, and just adding to all the crap that everybody else has given him throughout the day and at that moment I realized that I married a man that would lay down his life for another without a thought, the least I could do is be supportive and his rock instead of just being like everyone else he deals with at work. It is so hard to describe the feeling I had but it was like my heart became whole.

My whole attitude about my life as a police wife changed that day. I began to listen more and started to understand what his job was really like. I made sure that I did my best to keep the stresses at home to a minimum. I told him I loved him more. I learned to make random days special when I could. I learned how to be his safe place to get away from all the bad. You will hear many people say that this life, the police wife life, is like no other and it truly isn't, but it is what you make it. You get to choose to be that safe place for your husband and you should be very proud of that and, even more, you should be very proud to be a police wife. -Misty

Understand that life does not stop because you are a police wife. It just means that your life is going to be just a little more chaotic. It is important to make sure that you still care for yourself and make time to tell him about your day, your stresses or frustrations, and your good things. Just because he is a police officer doesn't mean it is all about him and his needs and his schedule all the time. It is okay to want and needs things to. He will understand this so don't be afraid to talk to him about it. Trust that your needs and wants are just as important to him and his are to you.

We married eleven days before one year of the first day we met. I will admit I thought I could do it. The first month of being married was so hard. We had bought our first house and our schedules were completely different. I remember thinking I had made a mistake because marriage was supposed to be a fairytale right. He would come home every night and eat dinner, he would be there for every holiday, etc. I remember not sleeping because I was so worried that he would get injured on the job and not come home. It wasn't until I gave it to God that I was able to release the anxiety that I felt every time the man I loved walked out the door. I realized no matter what, our lives had already been written. I knew where my husband was going if something bad were to happen and I never wanted to steel his joy. He loved his job and he loved me, there was room for the both of us.

The things I learned was to get involved in church, your kids school, your community, a hobby, or anything that strikes your interest. Be prepared to spend the holidays without him, birthdays, BBQ, school plays, etc. It has never been easy but it has been worth being with the man I love so dearly, and said I do to almost 18 years ago. The best piece of advice a friend gave me was that times will get hard and there will be times that you want to leave, there will be times of great happiness, and sadness, she said "Always stay committed to your commitment." I have lived by that advice for many years. -Denise

Here are a few other ways that your life may change after the blue, according to other wives:

- *We had more time together before but the time we have together after is definitely more meaningful.*

- *Before the blue, there was always the worry if he would be deployed again and the not knowing. He was home every night and only had duty days so often each month. After, we had to adjust to the crazy schedules and me having to go to the kids' activities alone a lot.*

- *I had a lot more friends before the blue. I could sit in a room without thinking about every bad situation possible.*

- *Holidays, birthdays, weekends, and fridays are all now on any day except the day that they actually are on the calendar. There is never a dull moment.*

These guys put their lives on the line every time that they leave for another shift. They never know exactly what they are going to see, hear, or deal with during each shift. Some days are quiet, with few calls while others seem to not even allow them a break to breathe and regroup. Sometimes the biggest issues arise before they even clock in, and life changes in the blink of an eye.

Writing this is like pouring salt into the wounds all over again. It was four years ago in June that my husband was on the way to work and he was run off the freeway by an unmarked Lincoln Crown Victoria going 100 mph. At first, he thought it was maybe a detective on the way to a call, maybe looking at his phone. My husband Steve called his old station he worked at as a Deputy Sheriff and asked them to run the license plate. When it came back to an average citizen he became more concerned about the way this car was driving and called California Highway Patrol. He told them that he thought the guy was a DUI suspect and that he was just run off the road by him. You would think that the call would end there, but this is just where the story begins.

CHP continued to speak with my husband about what the suspect was doing and where he was. They continued to reassure my husband that they had units rolling Code 3. The suspect pulled his vehicle over onto an on ramp of the freeway and stopped his car, my husband pulled over three to four car lengths behind him. He was still being told that CHP was rolling Code 3. The suspect got out of the car and started to walk towards my husband car with his hands in a fist. He began to back his car up to distance himself from the suspect. It was 3:30 am and he couldn't see if he had anything in his hands or not. The man finally figured out that my husband was not going to get out and fight him, and he got back in his car and took off. My husband continued to follow him at a distance. The man finally exited and my husband followed, still on the line with CHP and answering their questions. In the video you see the suspect go down the off ramp, cut off a van and blow a stop sign. My husband follows about 20 seconds later and makes the left. At this point the suspect has gone down under the freeway and made a

U-turn and starts driving his car in my husband's lane head on. My husband is still on the phone with CHP, at this point yelling "he is going to hit me", "he is going to hit me". My husband again puts his car in reverse to lessen the impact of the collision. At the last possible second the suspect swerves and begins to roll down his window. My husband fearing for his life thinks the suspect has a gun and fires several rounds into the suspects' car. The suspect takes off and of course my husband is still on the phone with 911 and has to follow the suspect, because he has been in a shooting. The suspect calls 911 and says some guy shot him and he doesn't know why, when the other 911 operator announces it is an Off-Duty Deputy. Great, right? The suspect wasn't interviewed for hours after being pulled over and taken to the hospital for his injuries. He was shot in the arm and had shrapnel in his eye.

It was a process of three years for him to be investigated by the Los Angeles District Attorney's office and cleared that included the suspect filing suit against the County and being awarded $975,000. Because of the suit Internal Affairs dragged their feet in wrapping the investigation up. On July 10, 2014 my husband was sent home. He texted me and I went into my bathroom and sobbed. When he got home, he broke down in my arms, so worried about what the future held. He got the papers ten days later that he was being fired.

Even though everything in our world was falling down around us, I was being positioned within several support systems that were pivotal in helping me survive that time. I had started going to a small Bible study, a prayer group that met twice a week, and had also found this cop wives group. I would not have been able to weather all of those storms in our lives without all of their support and my faith.

The week after my husband got the letter confirming that he was fired, he went out and got his commercial driver's license and began to drive an 18-wheeler across country. The kids and I would talk to him daily and we would see him every 5 weeks if we were lucky. He finally went to his first court hearing the following April in which the County put on their case, they talked about how well liked my husband was, that he worked for the depart for 26 ½ years, that he had outstanding reviews for the last 13 years, and he was asked to work at several different units throughout his career. Their shooting expert couldn't recall one thing from my husband's shooting review. Basically, they said that they were upset he had shot his gun in self-defense and could never back the policies that they fired him for.

In the meantime, we stayed so the girls could stay in their schools and be with their friends. We survived off my husband's excess vacation, sick and saved time. He realized in April that he was going to need to go to the oil fields to make a living and set off for Wyoming, not knowing when we would see each other again. In June our home sold and closed in late July. My kids, friends, and Crossroad Church all helped me pack to move to Wyoming where we found a home outside Yellowstone Park. In August, my husband went to his part of the hearing and the county had still not produced the 17 items that were subpoenaed months before. The arbitrator denied all my husband's request for evidence needed to defend himself. The county

*offered him a resignation and he took it, because his
attorney told him he would not be getting his job back.
Since my husband knew he was unable to get his
hands on any of the evidence and they had no intention
of reinstating him, my husband resigned and took his
retirement.*

*You may be thinking poor me or how awful, but
when I look back these are the things I am thankful for
1) Learning to lean on and trust God in all things, I
learned if you do his will you will be blessed beyond
measure, not always the way you want them to be, but
just what He knows you need. 2) I will be forever
grateful my husband came home to me in one piece over
four years ago. I feel so blessed to have not had the
burden my husband's step mother has had to endure
and that was the loss of his father in the line of duty
when he was 15. 3) That my marriage is solid and that
I will have my soul mate with me as long as the good
Lord gives us. 4) That my kids are resilient and have
loved and supported their Dad every step of the way,
even when they had to move from their home and
friends. 5) Feeling blessed by all my friends and
neighbors that stood behind us every step of the way.
For those who did not know me but loved me at my
weakest. 6) For the Christian women and men who
were there and just loved me where I was at in my
walk. 7) I am thankful for my beautiful home and the
vacation rental business in one of the prettiest places on
earth. 8) For all of my husband's partners and friends
who stood by him, knowing he was being railroaded. 9)
Most of all God's grace through all of this. He carried me
when I was weak and held my hand when I would*

begin to slip, He never let go.

Ladies I am not saying that life is all glitter and rainbows, but I am moving on the best I can. I am trying to forgive those that knew the truth and didn't speak it just to save their own skin. I am trying to forgive a job trade for a signature. It is something I will have to do to be whole again and move on. I pray often for all those who betrayed my husband. I know one day there will be a day of judgment. I am still a work in progress and a long way from perfect myself.

I just hope that you, as a police officer's wife, are really prepared for all the what ifs in this life. Ladies, invest in your marriages, be there for your husbands when he needs to talk, hug him when he needs a hug, and most of all enjoy your life because it can change in the blink of an eye. May the Lord keep your families and your husbands safe. This world is changing and it is so dangerous for those in uniform these days.

To the ladies in my Cop Wives Headquarters group thank you for being so loving and supportive through this time in my life. You will never know how much your kind words and your support meant to me in my darkest hours. The blue line family is an amazing support system. Thank you for always having my back.
- DS

This life requires a lot of patience, a lot of flexibility, a lot of independence, a lot of strength, and a whole lot of faith. We have to be ready to prepare for sudden changes in life and be willing to find our way through together. This life does increase safety risks to you and your family and there are plenty of people who have been arrested and locked up for their own decisions and yet they blame your husband because he was the one that locked them up. While our heroes do their best to keep their families safe and away from danger, they cannot plan for every possible scenario; sometimes you may get dragged into a dangerous situation when you least expect it.

We had just signed papers for the contract on our very first house. Leaving that meeting we were so excited about what was to come! We were getting married in two months and would close on the house two and a half weeks before the wedding. So I was going to move in right away so that I can get everything organized to my liking. He was currently a courtesy officer at an apartment complex that was not in the best area of town, but since he had been there, he had really taken care of a lot of the issues so did not have many calls to deal with. Everyone knew him and knew that he would handle business if they were screwing around.

We had stopped to vacuum out his Tahoe on the way back and while we both had our personal guns on us, while he was vacuuming, he moved them out of the way and I did not see where he put them. Normally, that would not be an issue, but this day was different.

We had pulled into the complex and were driving around towards the back and three guys were walking across the parking lot. So he rolled down his window, and asked them if they lived in the complex or who they were visiting. They rolled their eyes and kept walking. So he got a bit louder and more stern and told them that they needed to tell him who they were there with otherwise they needed to leave the premises because they were trespassing. One of them mouthed off to him, so he threw the Tahoe in park, and he jumped out. He had started walking over to them, explaining again who he was and that he needed them to answer him, otherwise he would call more officers and they could all go to jail for trespassing. They still just mouthed off, so he started to walk back to the Tahoe, to toss me his phone and tell me that I needed to go ahead and call dispatch. As he was almost up to the window, one of the guys came up behind him and shoved him.

My heart sank because I knew at that point the threat level had just greatly escalated and there were three of them. They had made it pretty clear about how they felt about respecting law enforcement and being compliant. He had taken hold of the one that shoved him and led him over to the grass to put him down so that he could keep control of him instead of putting him down on the asphalt. I was on the phone with dispatch at that point and they had already called out and sent two officers our way. In a matter of seconds, the situation turned bad. While he had the one on the ground, all of a sudden the other two came running up and jumped him, pushing him on the ground, which allowed the third one to get up, and it was three against one. My fiancé was on his back on the ground, and my heart hit the floor. My blood pressure maxed out I believe because all of a sudden I got angry.

I was furious that these three gang members were going to put my fiancé in danger and that was it. He had yelled for me to get his gun, so as I am telling dispatch that an officer is down and they needed to get help their fast, I was also searching for our blasted guns that he had put up somewhere while we vacuumed the Tahoe. I was going a bit crazy, yelling at dispatch that we needed help now and that I could not find our stupid guns! I am sure that that call into dispatch was a bit crazy. Then, I found our guns and with zero thought to what it may mean for me, I grabbed his gun, still had the phone to my ear, being held by my head to the side, and I threw my door open and jumped out with the gun and yelled "STOP! I have a gun!" as I drew down on the three of them. Well, I suppose the knowledge that this crazy white girl had a

*gun and none of them did, and while my hands may
have been shaking a bit (thinking I may have to actually
use the gun in order to save him, while making sure I
did not hit him), I was yelling and furious and they
knew it. So all of a sudden the three of them take off
running and I hear sirens, a lot of sirens, and M was
able to jump up. He comes and grabs the gun from me
and takes off after the three guys.*

*Then the calvary arrived. Officers from the Sheriff's
Department(his department), detectives, narcotics
officers, city police, and everything in between started
showing up because they were all going to come to
make sure that the officer down did not end badly. The
first one stopped next to me, asking me what had
happened and where they went; I told them and asked
them to please make sure he was ok. They had me
drive the Tahoe back to his apartment and then one of
the supervisors got out to stay inside with me and my
bonus daughter who was 4 at the time and had been in
the backseat.*

*The calvary spread out to apprehend the three guys
and they were able to get two of the three pretty
quickly. Later that night they were able to pick up the
third. However, one of the things we found out after
they caught the first two, is that all three were
prominent gang members and that retaliation from the
gang was very likely. Multiple supervisors and other
leaders were there at that point and they told us that,
for safety reasons, we needed to get all of his stuff out
of the apartment that night and stay somewhere else.
Their fear was that retaliation would happen when he
was working (he was on midnights at the time), and
that they would wait until his patrol car was gone. They
could potentially hit up the apartment while I was there
with the four year old. They said it just wasn't worth
the risk.*

So that night, we packed up everything. So many officers were coming in and out to help with whatever they could. One brought pizza and drinks and everyone helped pack everything up and get it out. That night was a blur. It made this life very real. In a matter of moments, everything changed. I realized exactly what I was getting into. I had done lots of ride alongs while we dated and were engaged, and those truly helped open my eyes to what he dealt with every shift. There had been calls that we went to that made me nervous for him, especially the domestic calls that he would get. Domestic calls are always the most volatile that the officers have to answer, so those were the ones that bothered me most. However, this day, that all changed. I saw what he was truly up against. For the first time, I saw people who had zero respect for law enforcement, that truly hated him for his badge, and were willing to hurt him for just asking them why they were walking around.

That night I held him tighter and didn't want him out of my sight, honestly. It made me nervous on his next shift but through praying a whole lot, I had a peace about everything; about sending him out to work, back out to the streets where he couldn't control everything, about our future, about being a cop's wife, and everything that entailed. I was ready to walk down the aisle(well the beach) and marry my hero, with my eyes wide open to what this life was going to be like. A myriad of emotions and worry over his safety ran through me, but I was committed to him, forever, no matter what, and being by his side through the good and the bad.

-Jess

Some of us come into this life slowly, we slowly learn what they have to deal with and what it is going to mean for us. We know that we love them too much to walk away, regardless of the challenges that we may face because of this life. They are too important to us to give them up. However, others are more aware of what it means to be around Law Enforcement Officers. That is because they are the dispatchers who send them out to each call and some are lucky enough to be the spouse of the same officer that they have to send out towards the danger.

For 30 years, I had the pleasure of telling Officers where to go. I was their mom. Their work wife. Their confidant. Their dictionary. Their lifeline. I loved them. Each and every one. Many I never met in person. But I loved them. They were my flock. Was it easy sending them into danger? Absolutely not. But this was the job, no, the career, both they, and I had chosen. They went where I told them. Even the one that I went home to after every shift. Was it even harder to send him into danger? The call was his. It was his beat. It was his job to go. It was my job to send him. Was it frightening to hear him say shots fired, I'm in pursuit, send me cover? Of course. But I trusted his ability. I trusted the Officers covering him. I had faith.

Being married to a Police officer means you are not only married to him, but you are married to his job. You are immediately expected to understand their stresses. Their hours. Their dedication. The laws! They go through months of training. Then they have a training officer do "on the job" training. They generally always have some type of supervision. Us. We have vows. Where's our training? We pretty much wing it. We learn as we go. On the job training. Whatever you call it, we do our very best to understand why they do not feel like talking when they come home after a really long shift. We try to understand why they cannot sleep, no matter how quiet we keep the house. Why they "can't turn it off" when they aren't on duty. Yes honey I do see that license plate is expired. They are a Police officer 24/7. Us. We are a wife. A mother. A worker. We wear as many hats as they do. Some days it's not easy doing all we do and then on top of it all, our husband comes home to us, thankfully, with his head full of things people should never have to see. Now what? Which hat do we put on? The wife wanting to tell them all about our day. About our work. About the children. Or are we the counselor. We know they need time to "decompress". Everything they deal with, where does it go? How do we as their wife help? How do we know when to speak. Or to stay quiet and give them time? We just learn. We have no training. We just learn. It's not always easy. Ok. It's always not easy. I had an advantage of knowing what he was doing at work the entire shift, of thinking I knew what he was dealing with, but when we got home at the end of that shift, I saw the effects of what he dealt with. Me. I was safe and sound. If anyone was yelling at me I could place them on hold. No one shooting at me. But him. He ran code with his lights and siren trying to avoid all the idiots not pulling over while going over scenarios in his head of how he was going to deal with this situation once he got there. Was his cover close? Was I giving him, as his dispatcher, all the information he needed? Was I painting the picture of the scene in his head so he could prepare? So. Even having the advantage of knowing what calls he went to, was not enough at times. He saw what I didn't.

The best advice I can give to a fellow law enforcement wife is just to love them. Let them talk. And really listen. If it has nothing to do with work, that's ok. Just really listen. There are things they deal with they don't want us to have to experience. They protect us from those evils. So if they don't share, it's ok. They aren't withholding. They aren't denying. They are protecting. At least in their minds. If they want to share.

*Just listen. That's all they ask. Don't judge. You were
not there. Just hear what they are sharing. It's not
always easy for them to share the visions they have in
their heads with others, especially the ones they want
to protect the most. If they are quiet. Let them be
quiet. Just be there. That means more then you know.*
*We sleep safely in our beds. And pray they come home
to us. So when they do, just be grateful. Love them. And
listen with your heart. ~B*

Starting out in this life is almost like being
initiated into some crazy sorority/fraternity that you
are excited to be in, but you really don't have a full
understanding of what you are actually, and willingly,
walking into! In no time, you begin to finally
understand the little comments and jokes that only
Cop Wives can truly understand.

*Being the wife of a law enforcement officer brings
with it a whole barrage of new experiences, the good,
the bad, the ugly, and the funny!*
Having said that, you know you're a Cop Wife when....
*.....there is almost (always) some kind of overtime every
week.*
*.....when you just laugh at the 'abnormal' - "Going to be
late babe, we're trying to find some guy who is
supposedly walking down the street in only his
underwear". (Yes, it really happened!)*
.....your needs have to wait until after he's off his shift.
*.....you're in public and he whispers a short command
to move, duck down another aisle, etc., because he's
keeping you away from someone he's arrested.*
*.....sometimes your hubby describes his job as a police
officer and other days he tells people he is simply a
garbage collector.*
*.....you buy him shirts one size larger than normal to
accommodate his off-duty weapon.*

.....*you know where all the guns are in the house (and how to load and shoot them).*

.....*pens, paper, and an occasional casing can be found in a normal wash, not to mention about ten thousand black socks! (I quit trying to match them up!)*

.....*you invest in black and blue craft materials to re-create your favorite 'Thin Blue Line' crafts!*

.....*he chooses where to sit in the restaurant and which seat to sit in at the table and you find it perfectly normal because he needs his back to a wall and his front to an exit.*

.....*you don't get upset that he can't hug or kiss you in public while in uniform. He's being professional and keeping you both safe!*

.....*you've invested in a good, expensive iron and a lifetime supply of starch!*

......*you hear the sound of velcro, and you breathe a sigh of relief, because it means he's home safe.*

.....*you hear the sound of the Taser being tested in the next room and know a new week is beginning.*

.....*you just smile and nod when people make the 'I better not speed when (insert your hubby's name here) is working!' comment. You'll hear that and its variations a million times.*

......*you are a master at keeping the house quiet and dark while he sleeps during the day, including noise machines, fans, black-out curtains, etc.*

.....*you have an alarm system and a dog; not to mention your own Glock in the nightstand.*

......*you don't assume the worst when they haven't answered your calls or texts for hours while on shift, they contact you when they can.*

.....*your idea of a good date with your husband/partner is a day at the range!*

.....*you call out traffic violations other drivers are committing when driving.*

.....*you're riding in the car with your husband/partner and think nothing about him pointing out the random*

*person walking down the street, while he says: 'That
guy is no good, I've arrested him twice.'*

*....your husband shouts at the TV while watching the
news or CSI and says, 'That's not proper police
procedure, they would never do that!'*

*......you talk in 10-code more than normal English
sometimes..."10-4 babe".*

*.....you know half the police department by their last
names.*

*.....you say your last name and people say they know
your husband.*

.....you've got a black and white in your driveway.

......you've been told that everyone lies!

*.....you know exactly how much you can speed over the
limit without getting stopped (not that I know from
experience.)*

*.....you don't call to find out why he's late because he's
rarely able to get home from work on time anyway.*

*.....you have a separate room/closet/storage for all his
police gear.*

.....you don't find cop/donut jokes very funny.

*......you always answer the question, 'Can you tell I'm
wearing my gun with this shirt?'*

*.....on holidays you always send extra food to the
department.*

*.....people contact you for advice about the law, asking,
"Hey, not sure if you husband can help..."*

*......you stay up later or wake up earlier just to see him
off to work.*

.....you know your exits.

*......you always have dress clothes ready and pressed
for court on his days off.*

*.....no matter how many times you've seen him uniform,
it still makes you swoon.*

*.....no matter how long the days/weeks/months can
get, you realize how proud you are, and how you
wouldn't trade this life for anything. ~M.S.*

This life is full of stereotypes, jokes and little humorous jabs that only us wives can truly understand. We often get a good chuckle trading stories, laughs, memes, etc., with each other but what about the tougher stereotypes of this profession? Such as the high divorce rate, infidelity, etc. Those are the ones that absolutely shake us to our core. What we may have said would never happen to us, all of a sudden is becoming our reality. The pain, devastation, confusion, loss, heartbreak, anger, and every emotion in between comes like a flood. That is repeated over and over again while you attempt to wade your way through it all and decide how you are going to proceed.

Oftentimes, our gut instinct, can't be beat, as painful as our instincts may be. Police Officers are trained to detect the smallest micro-expressions that may implicate that a suspect or witness is lying to them. Officers often use misrepresentations to get more information out of someone when being questioned, honing in on their own skills of deception. Now please don't misunderstand, most often they use those skills at work, not on their wives. However, some of us do know the pain of seeing them lie to us and assume that we are completely oblivious to the deception. What they don't tend to understand is that we have become experts at reading behavior, their behavior. Even a flash of hesitation, a split second mood change, after we question them about a credit card charge, a text, or phone call, tells us more than we want to know. Our heart breaks in that moment, our trust in our hero is shattered and our confidence along with it.

I was 15, a few months shy of 16 years old when I met my husband. Its sounds cliché but I'm pretty sure it was love at first sight. From the moment I met him we've been a couple. I knew I was going to marry him on our first date. We were married four years later. I was 19, he was 22. We were young! He had been a deputy about 6 months the day we married. He was so confident, you could even say a little cocky, very full of himself. He always looked sharp and handsome. I found his attitude to be very attractive, yet hated it at the same time. Even after we had lived together, he still gave me butterflies thinking about him when we were apart. A year or so into our marriage he worked a lot at night. Everything about him started to revolve around his job and the people he worked with. He started becoming closer to the officers and dispatchers than me. He would invite me to some get togethers every now and then. But I'm a complete introvert. You could say the other police wives were less than enthusiastic about me being there. I'm shy and awkward, and I was probably 10+ years younger than most of them. I did not fit in. Meanwhile my husband did and was always talking, laughing, and having a great time. I was usually playing with the kids or pets. Definitely not in their clique.

A couple of years later I found out we were pregnant with our first baby, a girl. We were so happy and scared to be first time parents. He worked evenings mostly and slept most of day. We didn't spend a lot of time together. I went to most of my doctor appointments alone. At the time, he was still a deputy working for the county, but he had applied for the city. He got hired on at the city and was to start his first day on Monday, March 5.

Well, our daughter had different plans. I went into

labor and she was born at 7 am Monday, March 5, the same day he was to start his new job. When our daughter was around a year old, I started getting suspicious of his behavior. He started buying new colognes and taking extra care of his hygiene and appearance. I started noticing unknown numbers on our phone bills. I questioned him but he assured me that they were nothing to be worried about. Several months after that it was just a normal day. He was getting ready for work in the bathroom. I had made lunch and was cleaning up the kitchen. He had left his phone on the bar.

It started to beep so I picked it up and it was a text that read, "Hey! Are you working?" The number was not programmed to a name. I took the phone into the bathroom and asked, "Who is this?" He had a look of shock and guilt on his face. He rolled his eyes, then has a look of disgust on his face, and says, "She just will not leave me alone!" I again say, "Who is she?". He responds with Allison. She was a dispatcher. I had heard him talk about her before but had always pictured her in my mind to be older and unattractive, someone he wouldn't be into. That's pretty much how he had described her in the past. I can remember my heart racing and feeling shocked. He says to me, "She keeps calling and texting." I asked him why he was talking to her at all. He yells at me, "BECAUSE SHE IS MY FRIEND!" I told him that you don't hide friendships. His only defense was to say that she had been texting and calling all the time and he just didn't want to hurt her feelings by asking her to stop. He had to leave for work right after that.

*While he was at work I did some investigating on
her. I checked old phone bills from the last couple of
months and there were hundreds of texts and phone
calls, but all of them were deleted off of his phone. So I
had no idea what the texts said and it made me crazy!
Then, I looked her up on social media to check out her
page so I could see what she looked like. There were
tons of memes and picture quotes that said things like,
"lights and sirens excite me" and "badge bunny here".
She was actually advertising that she was a badge
bunny on social media. I was shocked and I felt like
such a fool. I started getting extremely angry at this
point. I could not stop myself from scrolling through all
of her albums, each badge bunny pic making me feel
smaller and smaller. He came home from work and we
sat at the kitchen table to discuss it all. I asked him
what the text messages said. He said that they really
didn't say anything. I wanted to know why he would
delete all of them if they had nothing in them. Then he
told me that in one of the messages she flashed her
boobs at him. My heart sank. I immediately told him to
get his things and leave our house.*

*He packed up and left. I sat at our kitchen table
alone in our quiet house with a broken heart. I was
thinking so hard about why it was happening to me.
What was wrong with me? There were only two men in
my life that I trusted and respected at that time, my
husband and my dad. My husband had just deceived
me and shattered my world. We ended up talking about
it again. He said they were just friends and there was
nothing else to tell. At this point, I no longer trusted my
husband. I already had low self-esteem and after that*

blow I started thinking that I wasn't attractive, that I didn't have enough to offer and a number of other negative thoughts flooded my mind for days. She was perfect. But me? I saw myself as a simple person, focused on loving my family. It's just in my nature to be honest and loyal to the ones I love.

My husband really turned my life upside down for cheap attention from a cheap person. He said he regretted it, that he made a huge mistake and was genuinely sorry. I can remember fighting about it and him grabbing my shoulders and pulling me into a hug so tight we slumped together to the floor against our kitchen cabinets and we both cried. I decided at that moment I was going to forgive him, not immediately in that moment, but eventually. He wanted me to trust him again. He truly started to change after this into a great guy.

Several years later we had our son. It was a rough pregnancy but he was there for me every step of the way. He has grown into an incredible husband and dad. He tells me everything now and we have become best friends since that awful time. So in a strange, twisted kind of way you could say Allison, the badge bunny was a blessing in disguise. -Jerri Thomas

There are so many emotions on the opposite end of the spectrum when it comes to what our heroes and what we as wives have to deal with in this life. Sometimes it affects our marriage and our direct relationship with our husband. Other times it has to deal with the type of calls they have to answer and the images that are forever imprinted in their brains. Some days they are able to get through seemingly unscathed and others absolutely rock their world and are devastating.

Our husbands all have different calls that they have had to answer that they will never forget, that will always haunt them. Different reminders will immediately cause them to flashback to that house, car, building, etc. You could see it all over them when they finally got home after it. For mine, it was a murder-suicide call. A woman had been murdered by her ex-husband and then he had killed himself. Her newborn baby had been there with her.

It was an incredibly gruesome scene from what he told me, but one heartbreaking detail had stood out to him as soon as he arrived on scene. He noticed a laundry basket and on top was a pair of little girl's pajamas that seemed to have been freshly folded, now were covered in blood spatter. What made that stick out to my husband was the fact that they were identical pajamas to what our daughter had as well. This was his last call of the night. He came home afterwards and filled me in on a little. But I knew that as he laid there in bed with me, that all of those details from the crime scene were running through his mind. -Jerri Thomas

Our heroes have to see so much pain along with terrible and gruesome details on the job, from suicides, domestics that have gone bad, children that have been abused, kids that have been killed, drug addicts trying to hurt friends or family because they need their next fix, and so many awful scenes. Then they go back to the department, write up their paperwork on the case and head home. All of that pain, those horrible scenes, the vast number of emotions they went through during that one shift, they can't just shed it all off and forget it as they take their uniform off. Some of the cases stick with them, there will be some cases that seem to haunt them for a very long time. As wives, we have to figure out how to best help them. Sometimes they want to talk, they need to get it out of their head and share it with you. You don't have to fix anything, you just need to be there for him. You need to be his strength when he is overwhelmed, when he isn't sure how to handle something or what he needs to do, he needs to know that you have his back, that you are going to be there for him, no matter what. He needs to know that even on days he is working crazy late and you feel like you are not a priority, when he does get home and you know he is home safe, just let it all go. Be thankful that he made it home to you, and that he is safe, and just be there for him.

This life is not always fair for the wife. It can be extremely frustrating. While your husband loves you, he loves the kids, loves his family, there are going to be plenty of times that work comes first. That while he may have promised he was going to be home on time for dinner, giving y'all extra time to talk and just do something together that night, you are going to get a text five minutes after he was supposed to be home saying that he caught a case at the end of his shift, and it's going to be a while. Most likely your first reaction is going to be that of anger. You are going to get pissed off that he didn't make you the priority, that he broke his promise, again. We all know that sometimes, getting that text, or that same call, is infuriating. But here is the thing, your anger, it does zero good. Part of the life is being 100% flexible. You have to be willing to change your plans at the last minute, to accept that instead of six o'clock dinner, the two of you can eat at 11:30pm that night, or at least you can get out of bed and come sit with him while he eats that late. Just ask him about his day. He will be tired, he had to deal with more than he bargained for today. You were counting down the minutes earlier until he was going to be home because you had so much you wanted to talk to him about. But the night took a different turn. So you can get angry about it, cause a fight and division in your marriage because the night didn't go your way, and most people would tell you that you have every right to be angry; but most people don't understand this life. See, your husband, he didn't want to be late, he wasn't trying to stay away longer at work instead of coming home to you. He hated getting that case in the last 15 minutes of his shift, but it was his job to take care of it and so he went out and handled it. He knew by doing so he was letting you down and these heroes aren't trying to intentionally let us down. But it is going to happen. And how we respond is completely on us.

So the next time he gets stuck late at work or he comes home and you can tell it's been a hard day and he just isn't up for talking, be understanding. Don't get angry because you have to wait to share the things you were so excited to talk to him about, that you had to postpone dinner, realize that he needs you right then. He just needs your presence. He may not want to talk at all, that's ok. Just be there. Hold him if that's what he needs. Let him lean into you, and forget about all that he had to see that day. Put your needs aside and understand that you can wait until tomorrow, but he needs you then. So be there. Be whatever he needs.

This life is not easy. Our guys hold a lot of stuff in, internalizing pain, fear, and so much more. The longer they are on the job, if they can't find a good outlet, a way to decompress, they are going to withdraw from you, stop talking to you about the cases he is dealing with, stop making time for you. It's normal to get mad, hurt, frustrated, and many other things. It's hard when you feel them withdrawing from you, and you aren't sure how to fix it. That is when you have to be willing to fight for them, to fight for your marriage. Our marriages take a beating in this life. There is so much darkness that attempts to stick to the guys and then gets brought home into our marriages and our families. We have to fight to get it out, to make our marriages and our families sacred. They need to know that regardless of what has happened, that we haven't given up on them. That we are there for them, to support them with anything they are up against. You do not have to be a statistic of this life, losing your marriage. It is worth fighting for and getting through whatever darkness has crept in.

There is a reason that the divorce rate runs so high with this profession Law Enforcement Officers see the worst of the worst, day in and day out, and the longer that they are on the job, the more that they are taking in. Evil and darkness try very hard to begin seeping through people, coloring their experiences, and targeting their worst fears and bring them face to face with their biggest aversions. Our heroes often try to not bring work home, to shelter us from the darkness that they walk in throughout their 12 hour shifts. Ladies, that is what will change your husband, and not only change him, it will also change you. We are deeply and unconditionally in love with our man and that leaves us very tuned in to his moods and feelings. When he comes home from an incredibly hard case, needing to decompress, and attempt to process what he had to deal with, often times they withdraw from us. As they go for supposed decompressing time in another room, or outside on the porch, or wherever, and we leave them alone, thinking that is what they need; I think we get that wrong a lot of times. Oftentimes, when they are out sitting on the porch with a few beers, acting like they want nothing to do with us, the kids, or anything else in life, that is when we need to make certain that they know we care, we love them, and that we are always there for them, no matter what. How do we accomplish that? Set down whatever it is you are working on, packing lunches, finishing up the dishes, etc., and just go out there, sit on the porch swing with him. Take his hand, cuddle up to him, put your arm around him and just tell him that you are there for him, always. Let him know that if he needs to talk, you want to listen. If he needs to just sit and be quiet, you want to sit and be quiet with him.

So many times we allow their standoffish and withdrawn behavior to tell us to just leave them alone, to give them their space for a while, that he will come to you if he needs to. We have got to start remembering that they are just a person, tasked with a massive and unending job to do, and they can get overwhelmed with it all. They can be just as bad as we are about opening up and being honest with how they are feeling or what they need in a given moment. So we need to stop making them always come to us. There is nothing wrong with meeting them exactly where they are. Be the initiator to remind him of how important he is to.

Being part of this blue family, well it's kind of like parenting, it's the best worse job ever. There are so many amazing things that we get to be a part of, that we get to experience with our #BlueHeroes. They are strong and confident, they are willing to fight for those that can't fight for themselves, they will run towards the danger when everything in their body is yelling to turn around and run away from it! It makes us so proud to see them suit up, to know that they love what they do, they are proud of their job, and they want to serve and protect their community, even at the expense of their own safety. We can't help but be so proud of them. We may not tell them that enough, but we should. They need to know just how much we love them, how proud we are of what they do, that we will stand by them always. On the flip side, there is a lot of unknowns, fear for their safety, attempting to understand and predict if they need us to talk to them or just be there and be quiet, letting them know with our presence that we support them. This life is hard, but it's amazing. There is nothing that makes us smile more than to see our sexy hero all geared up and ready to go make a difference. Then to hear him get home after shift, and that places your heart at ease. You have to be willing to make his life, to make his job, your life. That is the only way that this works. It is full of sacrifice and figuring out on a whim what he needs from you most. It's not easy but not one of us would want any other life because it is the best/worst life in the worl, and it has our heart because he has our heart.

4 Why We Do It

If this life is so crazy, with missed holidays, dinners, date nights, etc., why in the world would any of us choose this life? That is a complicated answer. It's not an answer that is consistent, it can vary depending on what we are dealing with. On a day that he sends several texts during his shift to check in, be sweet, let us know he is thinking about us, well on those days we think this life couldn't get any better! Then there are days that you don't hear from him at all, your texts have been ignored, the dinner you spent time making for him is sitting on the stove and counter getting cold because he is already an hour late and still hasn't called, On those days you are ready to fight someone and you have no clue why you signed up for this craziness. The later it gets that frustration changes to worry, so when he opens the door you are so relieved that he is home safe, everything else flies out the window. That uniform sure gets them out of a whole lot of trouble with us wives!

We do this because we were called to it, just as our heroes were. Once you step into this life, you can't step back out. It becomes part of you. While it's not easy, you learn how to deal with different aspects and no longer let it phase you. It makes you strong, it makes you learn how to fend for yourself because they are on the job so much, so you become much more independent. It makes you grow as a person, you have to deal with things that normal people don't. You get used to the odd hours, the texts that say he will be late, having a special night with your hero when his phone goes off and you know exactly what that means. He has to go suit up to go and handle a situation, or go and help a victim. It hurts to see him go, to see him have to leave when the time was supposed to be for the two of you but you understand. It's just how your life is. The two of you will have to make up for it later, somehow.

Some nights I hit the pillow, exhausted by the day. A little text to say "I love and miss you. Be Safe." And I fall right to sleep. I love those nights.

Other nights I lay awake. Tossing and turning, worrying, trying to be super-mom, but feeling like failure-mom. The kids need picked up while neither of us are available. Who can I call this time? The bills are stacked on the table from last week. Kids' messes, his messes, my messes everywhere. Something else is broken? Great. Just great. That'll never get fixed. Oh, my lawn is too tall and the roses need pruned. I need to get to work early to catch up on that project I'm behind on. Oh geez, I didn't get anything out to thaw for dinner. When did the kid need lunch for that field trip? I hope it's not tomorrow. Is it hot in here? Who turned the thermostat up!? OUCH! Stepped on a dog chew! I need a drink of water. Now I need to go to the bathroom. Oh good, it's raining again...can't mow the lawn...again.

Maybe I'll text him and see what he's doing. No response. I play a game on my phone. Twenty minutes later, still nothing. Turn on my scanner app. Listen for his voice and number. Nothing. My heart beats a little faster. All the scary things begin to run through my head. Then I hear his voice. He's been out with a

*domestic. One in custody and on his way to the jail. In
that moment all the little problems in my life don't
matter. I just need to know he's safe. And he is.*

*People ask me if I worry about him and my first
answer is always no. I say he knows what he's doing,
he's trained well. He makes good and safe decisions.
But deep inside I do worry at times. He's out there with
people who hate him for what he does for a living.
People who are crazy. People so drunk or strung-out on
drugs they don't know what they're doing. People that
could take him from this world.*

*My worry is my little secret. It's just a tiny little thing
that sits in my heart. I don't go there often. I can't go
there often. It would destroy me. I can't let the kids see
me worry. Must. Be. Strong.*

*With all the stresses that come with being a mom and
wife, add police wife and some days we are to our limit.
It is a great balancing act. And sometimes we are truly
putting on an act to just make it through. And that's
okay. We do what we have to do. One day at a time.*

*So as you can see, I had a sleepless night. I'm
exhausted, my back hurts. Once again he came home
safe to me today. My worries did nothing but make me
tired and need a second cup of coffee this morning. But
he doesn't get to know that. I will not burden him with
my worry, although I'm sure he knows. He knows me
well. I love him for that.*

*I guess the moral of my story is that it's okay to
worry, but don't let it consume you. We are always
going to worry about the people we love. We are going to
worry about work, the house, our kids. But laying down
at night and worrying is just bad for us! It accomplishes
nothing and we have a rough next day. Find a way to
not let yourself go there. Meditate, pray, take a bubble
bath before bed. We are the glue of our families and we
must remain strong! So rest your pretty little head my
fellow night worrier and just sleep. ~ Amy T.*

As Law Enforcement Officer Wives, we have to learn how to be the pillar of strength for our hero, which means keeping some of the worry and frustration with the job to ourselves. Not to hide anything from them, simply to keep any extra worry and stress off of them. It is our job to try and make our home their safe place. They need to be able to walk through the door and be able to take a deep breath and instantly relax, to know that you are there for them. It's our job to help them decompress after their shift, to be there to either listen to what they had to deal with that day/night, or to simply be there with him. Words are not always needed. Their law enforcement career can change, their responsibilities can shift, and that is going to cause a shift at home. We have to learn how to roll with those changes because we are their support, their safe place, and because we love them no matter what. This job becomes their life and in turn it becomes ours.

When I walked eyes wide open into this life, he was on midnight shift patrol. So we were on completely opposite schedules, he worked Saturday night, Sunday night, Monday night, and Tuesday nights. I was working Monday-Friday and would get off between 3-5pm. So our time together was very limited. We made a priority to make time for each other. And that is so very important. This life can overwhelm and completely take over your time if you are not careful and are not proactive to make each other a priority. So for us, when I got home he would still be asleep. I would wake him up a little later after I had dinner ready, he would shower, we would have some time together, he would eat, and then he suited up, kissed me, and headed out the door. It wasn't easy, but we made it work. Our time together was short, but it made it that much more special.

I got pregnant with our daughter about six months after we were married. I was so excited to be pregnant with her. Around the same time, he had a friend who decided to run for Sheriff of another county and wanted him to come be a detective if he was elected. Fast forward to August of 2010, his friend was elected and he turned in his resignation and became a new detective. I had reservations about the job change. I was afraid it wasn't going to pan out like it was being promised. However, one thing I learned pretty quickly being married to him(probably a LEO trait), was that I could speak my mind, give my opinion on something if I felt that he was wrong on something, or choosing the wrong path, I would let him know that I didn't think it was the right thing for him/for us, but he was the head of our home, and ultimate decisions fell to him. Me pushing a point and keeping him from doing something he wanted to do(even if I knew it wasn't a great idea) would have just caused more problems, leading to being blamed for missed opportunities. So after speaking my piece, if he still disagreed, then the outcome was on him.

He went into this detective position saying that he would be working 8-4pm and would finally be home more but I knew better, I was not stupid. I was absolutely right. He got called out all of the time. Once during one of the girl's birthday parties, we were getting ready to cut the cake, and he got called out for a murder. That is great party conversation! That became a common theme. He would work his 8-4pm, get home, and later that night he would get called out for something else. So while I had been used to the crazy schedule and us missing each other often, this detective life was way different. Mainly because there was only two, including him, for the entire county. So I got even better at doing life, doing home, doing the kids on my own, and not counting on him being there, but if he was able to be, then it was a pleasant surprise! That is a big thing to remember in this life- do not have big expectations of him. You will continue to be disappointed. Most of the time it will not be his fault. So get rid of the expectations and you will be so much happier and more content in this life. They do not need a clingy, needy, wife. They need a partner, a support for what they have to face day in and day out.

Detective lasted about 7 months, then he got accepted into law school, so he transferred back to his old department as an SRO so he could attend law school at night. That was a long four years. That is what he wanted so I supported and encouraged him. If we thought he wasn't home a lot before law school, he really wasn't around much with school. That is two extremely stressful activities to have to deal with and especially doing it at the same time. This life, the job, does affect our heroes. After seeing so much hate, gruesome details, broken victims, dealing with family members who lose a loved one, it changes them. They become cynical, they don't trust people, and they stop understanding people who are optimistic and positive about life.

Let's just say that makes married life hard when your backgrounds are so different. I came from a big, close knit family, grew up in church and my faith remained my priority. I grew up naïve about a lot of things in life, he was my education on what he felt people were truly like. He did not grow up like I did. Then the fact that he had already been in law enforcement when we met, well, he was already somewhat cynical and my more optimistic view on situations would at times drive him crazy. He would tell me I was just living in a fantasy world. Believe me, that isn't easy to hear or to deal with. To have the person you love the most, feel that you just didn't get how life really was. So how are you supposed to deal with that?

If that's how things are, why do you do this life?

Because you do love him, you did make a lifelong commitment to him, and when you take into account what he is dealing with every day, it makes sense. I did love him absolutely and unconditionally, I made a lifelong commitment to him. So I had to remind myself why he had gotten hard. Why he was so much more cynical and short tempered with not only me, but with our girls as well. Our girls picked up on it easily and began walking around on pins and needles with him, afraid that they would do something to make him angry. I knew how they felt. Talking to him didn't always make a difference because I couldn't understand what he was going through. What do you do, how do you handle that?

If your hero starts to show signs of being bothered more easily, short tempered, cynical, blaming you for simple things that before never would have angered him, he needs someone to talk to. Just like we have encouraged you to find that support system, to find that group of women to truly understand what you are going through, he needs the same thing. He needs at least one person, someone older, wiser, who can help guide him through what he is dealing with. I think that too many people in general feel that counseling and talking through things is for the weak. For police officers, they are so used to always being in control, having the authority, it can be difficult for them to let their walls down. But if your marriage means anything to you, you need to make this a priority. You need to make your husband on the same page so that you can be proactive to issues that may arise from the job and in your marriage.

We all do this, because we love our hero, more than anything in life, and being his partner, his support system, walking this life with him, is absolutely worth all of the sacrifices. Make sure that you tell your husband that. He needs to know how much you love him, how proud you are of him, how you are willing to always be by his side, fighting whatever comes up, and you will work to keep your marriage the priority no matter how hard that may be with this life. You have to be on his team and make sure he knows that. This life gives more than it takes. We have found a sisterhood unlike any other, a support system to help us get through the hard days. We not only have a hero, we all got to marry our hero and no one will ever come close to him. -Jess

This life has a myriad of challenges that we all have to face day in and day out. Some are very obvious, the crazy schedules, the call outs, missed dinners, skipped parties and holidays. Other ones, we try not to focus on and people who are not in this life, do not understand at all. That is the safety issues that each of these officers are faced with. It's not only on duty, they are a target these days even when they are off duty and attempting to live life normally, but they can't. We can't live life normally. Of course we have safety concerns when they are on duty; we never know what they are walking into on a call, anyone could be angry enough to shoot at a cop, or put them in danger. But what about when they are off duty? What about having to do a gun check before you leave the house or you get out of the car; meaning that he asks you to ensure that you can't see his gun under his shirt. He knows that with as many people that he has arrested and locked up, they could want to hurt him. Unfortunately, they are no longer the only ones. These days you never know who in a crowd could hate Law Enforcement and be willing to hurt or kill an off duty officer simply because he wears a badge for his job.

"I don't know how you do it," some say. To be honest, there are some days I don't know how either,

other than I just do. I'm not a rookie cop wife, nor am I a veteran. I fall in the middle of this crazy unpredictable life. My husband and I have been together since college, married nine years. He has been in law enforcement for eight years and was in juvenile corrections a year prior. So pretty much, this life is all we know in our adulthood and married life. I had no way of knowing what was ahead, but was and still am committed to being supportive every step of the way. So many changes take place in the LEO life, at least in my experience, that you can't exactly prepare for until you live it yourself. My husband puts his all into his career. He doesn't do it for the status, he doesn't try to slide through each shift getting into as little as possible, and he doesn't just write his tickets and go home. He takes his career very seriously. He wants to be in the middle of things and he is confident in his ability to do his job well, to make a difference without being arrogant. He doesn't believe in being complacent as that makes you more vulnerable, and vulnerability can lead to him not making it home. I am very proud of him, but it does all come at a cost.

There's first of all the obvious ones: long hours, overtime, dinner breaks cut short, working holidays, nights, and weekends, missing family and social functions, etc. All of these things were expected when entering this life, but can still be frustrating and hurtful at times. Then, there's that internal change within your LEO after working the beat long enough to no longer trust anybody. Initially, it's the change of packing heat everywhere he goes, scanning every big crowd even at church, sitting facing the door at restaurants, that type of stuff. Eventually, the coldness starts to sink in. They've dealt with so many criminals and ugly situations that it's hard for them to find good in people. Their once laid back personality with a love for people is no longer present. They'd rather do their own thing most of the time and can be distant and hard to talk to. It may be an inevitable change for them when the public is constantly trying to pick them apart, sue them, hurt them, or worse, kill them or their family. It is scary to think there are complete strangers out there that would take a gun to my family just because my husband is a cop, a protector and server. It's almost as crazy to think how many women would like to get with my husband, too, because of his job. One extreme to another in this life.

Then, there are the tragedies. My husband sometimes closes his eyes and sees all the messed up things he's witnessed in his career...mangled bodies from a car accident, bodies inside of homes, lives destroyed by drugs, moms and dads torn up over the loss of their child, etc. . How can it not change a person? After all, cops are real people with real feelings and families although it seems many people seem to forget that. Because of the changes in my man, I'm changed, too. As much as I try to be the constant rock in his life, be his outlet, keep our home his safe haven, and be supportive no matter the circumstances, I mess up. I've had feelings of anger, resentment, bitterness, jealousy, loneliness, anxiety, and fear.

What helps me get over those rough moments? For one, prayer. Lots and lots of prayer. Two, having real conversations with my husband about these things. I will say it took hitting almost rock bottom personally for this to take place. I was too scared and upset to have the talks that needed to take place, but for ones' marriage, sanity, and peace, communication and trust are a must. Finally, reading stories of police wife widows help bring everything back to proper perspective. Oh how they'd love to have their last moments with their hubby back, how they'd love to find equipment and smelly undershirts in a big pile in the bedroom, how they'd love to hear "sorry, Honey, I'm going to be late" as long as it meant they'd eventually

return home. Their stories are reality checks and wakeup calls to the aggravations I endure. While I feel like a single mom some days, they are living it every day. Their perseverance is an inspiration to the rest of us, and I hope and pray I never have to go through that "change." Keeping that in mind, I will continue to be my husband's #1 supporter, stand by him, be his prayer warrior, and love him unconditionally no matter the circumstances. I hope when I become a 20 year veteran LEOW, I can look back on these days and see how much we've grown through the roller-coaster of life.
~ Lacey

We love our heroes. We understand that there are a lot of sacrifices that have to be made. We have to take on fear, anxiety, unknowns, frustrations, insane schedules, trying to be everything he needs us to be, in order to support him. Even knowing all of this now, after being in this life for years, we would make the same decision over and over again. We would always choose him and we will always choose this life.

So how do we do it? I firmly believe that the reason we do this is out of love for each other, which means loving each other's passions and calling. I also firmly believe that the only way this works, is if you both truly love all people. We are doing this out of unconditional love for all people, regardless of if the news, politicians, or the community believe that he truly loves them. I know he does and that is what matters. He wants nothing more than to serve and protect. He does not want to cause harm or cause pain; you simply cannot sacrifice this much if you are not doing it out of love. Now that love can become jaded, but ultimately to be a cop in today's world, you must have unconditional love.

This is really hard on marriages though, and it's important to truly understand this. People will play this down and often do. This job will cause your family to sacrifice a lot and it will change all of you. It will add a lot of trials, challenges, stress, anxiety and discomfort to your marriage. It will challenge your spouse's faith as well as his sense of peace. But ultimately, falling back on love is what makes it work. And I don't mean the tv version of love that is superficial; I truly mean falling back on unconditional love for each other and for the community.

You need that love in order to spend your weeks alone, handle watching him have nightmares & not being able to wake him up, stomach hearing about him get in a fight with gang members with no one to back him up except for federal agents at an office, miles away. You need that love to not bite your friends' heads off when they compare your husband never being around with their husband being home after 6pm occasionally. You need that love to deal with him coming in so exhausted and emotionally drained, and not having enough left to give you any attention. You need love to deal with the pain you see in his eyes about the horrible things he has seen, had done to him and had said to him all day, every week, for years. You need that love to deal with the unpredictability and insecurities. That love and faith is all that holds us together, and while I spend most days wondering why we do this for no money, little public support, and so much hatred towards my husband because of his job, unconditional love is what makes it all possible. - Michelle

I married into the "cop wife" life. When I met my husband he was already a detective and a marine. There are days where I honestly don't know how I do it but somehow I push through. Two years ago my husband was the responding sergeant to what ended up being a pipe bomb that went off in s garbage can in Seaside, NJ. I remember my phone starting to go crazy with texts and calls from friends asking if my husband was okay. I had not been on social media so I had no idea what was going on. I of course tried calling my husband's cell & he did not answer. Luckily, I'm friends with a dispatcher and reached out to him. I asked if Mike was okay & he said yes, he's just extremely busy. It turned out the entire pipe bomb hadn't fully detonated so they had their hands full. He was okay so I was okay. It was the scariest few minutes of my life.

I remembered thinking how do I do this? How do I live this life? What about my son if something happens to his daddy? The answer was simple. Someone has to do it, and that someone is my husband. He's tough, brave & so smart. He's the police officer, the marine, the man you want handling this situation because it will get handled the right way. My husband ended up being on scene commander in Seaside. It turned out to be an act of terror. What a scary world. But guess what? The next day my husband put back on his badge & did it all over again. When people ask me if I worry about him every day...I answer yes, but I don't let it consume me. I know my husband is the best kind of police & I know he will do everything to get home to me & the boys every night. Yes, our lives are hectic, crazy & the phone calls don't stop, but I wouldn't have it any other way. This is the life we chose. I will always be the wife behind the badge supporting him until our last day together. -Cathy

Most of us would say that we never envisioned

ourselves marrying a cop. They have the whole uniform thing going for them, which may be a nice passing thought, but for most of us the other aspects of the job, when dreaming of what our married lives would look like, a cop's wife didn't necessarily make the top of the list. We didn't dream of having missed dinners, doing birthday parties on our own, living moment to moment due to them getting a last minute call on shift. Yet we were drawn to these men. We each saw something in them that we couldn't help but find out more. Our heroes are willing to sacrifice everything for a greater cause, to truly serve their communities in whatever way they can. And they are a special breed, they were made for something more, something greater than what is normal. We know that being at a desk, doing mundane tasks would never satisfy them, and would never allow them to utilize their full potential. So we go all in, supporting whatever they choose to pursue and train for.

I didn't marry a cop. I don't know for sure how I got to be where I am today considering that I married a millworker. I was seventeen and desperately in love with this 24-year-old who had previously been an E.M.T. and a firefighter, among many other things. One thing he was not, however, was a LEO.

It was only a few months into our marriage that I began to realize that working at a mill on the Oregon coast was quite honestly a joke. He was so talented in so many ways; he had a strong work ethic and picked up new skills quickly and efficiently. He had so many strengths and apparently no weaknesses in the work place. I felt strongly that his life was basically being wasted working in a mill, although I had never fully prepared myself for where we would be in ten years.

*The mill laid off all workers after a few years and
we were stuck at rock bottom. We ended up in Alaska
and he was doing any odd job he could find. He
excelled as a wrestling coach, a paraprofessional at the
school, and he worked at the harbor. Somehow I still
felt like he had a greater job to do. He is one of those
people that is just meant for something special, like he
is bursting with untapped potential to do whatever he
wants and I could see that in him.*

*He became a dispatcher at the police department
and picked up on everything fairly quickly as usual. He
already had some experience since he had done first
responder work before. This was probably even easier
to do here, because our town is so small. There are only
about 800 people here during the winter, and the calls
are fairly mundane.*

*We settled into village life with Josh still picking up
work where he could and we consistently faced
unemployed summers. Work is highly seasonal here
and so summertime is when you have to take what you
can for work. I knew God wanted better for us and that
He had a bigger purpose for my husband, so I took to
praying about it. I kept thinking about how much better
off we would be if he were a firefighter again, or an
E.M.T. He could do either of those and I would be
happy. The pay would be good and he would be doing
what he was made for. I would be extremely proud to
show him off to everyone as my husband, the
firefighter. Or my husband, the E.M.T. It never ever, not
even once for even a second, crossed my mind that he
could potentially be a police officer someday.*

I still remember him telling me that the chief of police, a close friend, wanted him to do some type of law enforcement job. They needed a "seasonal officer" to take care of things for the summer and pick up the slack. I was taken aback to be honest. It simply didn't make sense that an average person with no training could just suddenly jump into any type of law enforcement job. I had no idea what it would entail or what it would really mean. I couldn't comprehend where the line would be drawn for what he was responsible for. When I finally gained somewhat of an understanding of what we were looking at, I didn't want him doing this type of work at all. It just wasn't what I had been praying for. I wanted him doing a safe job that I could be proud of. And after losing two officers in the line of duty in our tiny village in 2010, I realized that there is no "safe" place to be a LEO. Why would I want my husband getting involved in a job with so much more at risk?

He was given his own car and wore a uniform and everything. It was strange seeing him doing this kind of work! He assisted other officers and took care of the "grunt" work – like catching loose dogs and reading to children at the library. He also went on many calls and learned a lot about the career. Many people in town said he wasn't a "real" cop and was simply a dog-catcher. It was so disheartening to hear words like this. He was strictly instructed to wear his vest every time, especially dealing often with drunks and people brawling. There was no denying that he was putting his own life in danger every time he put on the uniform. I had his radio on at home and was listening in every night when he was working. It was usually pretty mild and I adopted this mindset that it was not in my hands. Everything had to be put in God's hands as it were. Did I trust the Lord with my husband's life? Because honestly, no amount of my worrying would keep my husband safe. Nothing terrible had happened so far and I began to settle into the idea that I was worried about nothing. At one point, I would even say I was fairly comfortable with the work Josh was doing. I was proud and bragged to people about his job and even though it was rough on the family for him to work late nights, it was an income and he seemed to be made for this.

I will never forget the first call that really scared me. I don't even remember how I heard what had happened but I remember packing up the kids and going down to my friend's house which was directly across the street from where it happened. Maybe I heard it on the radio, or maybe my husband texted me. He had been driving with his partner when a woman hanging off the balcony of the nearby lodge was shouting that someone had a gun. A man walking by on the sidewalk was the culprit, and they had to apprehend this man at gunpoint. It resulted in a minor bust, where several migratory workers were keeping alcohol, drugs, and unauthorized weapons.

I had totally let my guard down that there would ever be a dangerous situation. I didn't see how they could send my husband out there night after night when he wasn't really a cop, as the neighborhood had expressed. He must be some random person in a police car taking notes and wearing a Kevlar vest – because that's all I had emotionally signed up for. After that night, every call terrified me.

I'd stay up all night listening to his radio just to hear his voice. When something serious would happen, I'd frantically text him to make sure he was okay. Of course, if it was a serious call, I would spend hours waiting for that return text. I'd lay in bed and cry thinking "He's going to get killed. It only takes a split second to shoot a cop in the head and that's what's going to happen and I'm going to be raising all our children alone because someone is going to kill him." When I'd finally hear the dogs become restless and I heard him walk in the door, I could succumb to the sleepiness and fall in to the lullaby of his Velcro coming off and the gun locker opening and closing. I began to debate to myself if I could ever commit to this, because I couldn't make the fear go away. I longed for it to be over with and for us to move on, but at the same time I craved even more. I wanted so badly for him to make a career of this and for his full potential to be realized. I was teetering on the brink of loving and hating what he had become.

His temporary position was just that, temporary. We had it dangled in front of our faces that they needed a full time officer. We were elated at the opportunity but trying not to get our hopes up. We had conceived for several months that this was a door opened by the Lord and that this is where He was directing us, but we didn't know if it was meant to be permanent. We prayed and prayed, and waited and waited. We were told they would know "by next month" or "by next week" or "by Monday." Eventually it was given to someone else entirely. Some random people were brought in from out of town and I didn't know if I was relieved or disappointed. At times I felt betrayed but humbled. I didn't really know how I should feel at all. I would still dredge up those feelings to myself that this is not what I prayed for, this is not what I wanted. I could see the longing on my husband's face though. He was missing something. He wanted something more. My own feelings probably got in the way for him, because what I wanted out of it was still unclear to me. He struggled with his emotions about how badly he wanted this. There was nothing I could do for him either.

The next season came and the department turned to Josh for a reserve officer. He was able to put in quite a bit of time and it made him happy. I still found myself constantly annoyed at the few people making ridiculous remarks about him being a "wannabe" cop. As far as I was concerned, he was always just as likely to be shot in the line of duty as anyone else. At what point does it become real? Is it dependent upon his given authority? His training? His commitment to the job? The situation surrounding us taught me something I would have never known otherwise. People who don't live the life can't understand. It's not a job. It will encompass everything you have in you and everything around you. It becomes a lifestyle whether you want it to or not. I couldn't look at anything subjectively because everything is about my husband being a cop. I pledged that would never look at any officer the same way again. His best friend was his partner, who did not uphold a good relationship with the people in town. The people here are not fond of "outsiders" in any sense, and many of them have issues with white people. Add to that the fact that he was very strict and serious about his job and he was immediately labelled unfavorable and unfair. He had many death threats against him and many complaints, and it was Josh's job to keep him out of trouble and keep him safe despite the public backlash. This raised all new concerns for me. Why was my husband, the one officer without formal training, being charged with keeping this other person out of harm's way? Josh kept telling me not to worry. He was an expert at diffusing situations and keeping things from escalating. This is true of him, but it never really eased my mind in any way. He never let on that he was stressed, overburdened, or overwhelmed in any way. I was probably the crappiest support person ever at this point, mostly because I was stuck in a limbo between my husband absolutely being a real cop despite the naysayers, and yet wondering why he was doing real police work when I didn't marry a cop.

I had my mind made up one day after listening to something my dad said. My dad is one of those rude, gruff men. He won't compliment you. It kills him to say thank you or that he loves you. You really have to just read his tone and listen for deviations from his normal verbiage to understand what emotion he is feeling. One day my dad and I had several tourists that we were taking on a fishing trip. They were standing around in the parking lot and I will never forget their faces when Josh parked his police car next to us and got out. They just stopped talking and were frozen! It was one time that I became so aware that police are for some reason very intimidating no matter what they say or do or what they look like. He walked up to me and we started discussing when I would be back in town from the *fishing tour and when he walked away, my dad turned to the silent tourists. The tone of his voice as he spoke is so deeply etched into my memory. He told them "That's my son in law! He's a cop. He's my son in law...."*

There was so much pride welling in him to tell those tourists! I realized that it wasn't just me; everyone who knew about this whole endeavor was proud of what Josh was doing. It made me feel more committed than ever to my husband pursuing this career despite my reservations about the fear and the dangers. We mutually agreed that this is what we wanted – for Josh to be a full time and fully-fledged police officer.

Josh lost his reserve officer status at the end of 2014. The department appeared to be falling apart. The chief was harassed to the point of defamation and two of the officers were very unfavorable to the town. That left almost no one in good standing with the community at the department since there were only four officers total besides the reserves. The whole department was on the verge of being replaced and they once again began dangling a full time position in front of us, although I didn't have high hopes for it to work out this time any more than last time. The "we will know by _" date kept getting pushed back and we had to come to terms with the fact that this may not be what God had in store for us after all. Josh couldn't stifle his disappointment that we may have to move back to Oregon and that all the work he had put in would be for nothing. I went over it in my mind constantly trying to decide if I had, all along, wanted to return to the life that was normal to us – or if I would lament the loss of a new life we had barely begun to grasp. We prepared to leave in October when the Alaska PFDs would arrive, and I started looking at jobs in other towns out of state that may offer entry level positions where he could get sent to an academy.

The police department had a total makeover, replacing the chief and two officers almost overnight. I was disheartened to see our friends and my husband's coworkers leaving, but the new faces of the department were refreshing and the dynamic seemed much more conducive to what they were meant to accomplish. Josh was still dispatching and got to know all the new officers and he seemed to be once again longing to do that same work. News travelled down that they were wanting to hire at least one more officer, and I didn't hold my breath. I found out later that many people in town were pulling for Josh to be their first choice and the new chief all but promised Josh that he was first on their list if funding went through for another officer. Some days they would say it was looking very positive for Josh, and other days it didn't look like it would work out. We spent several weeks just praying for God's will because we didn't know what to even hope for anymore.

It came all of a sudden and out of the blue that Josh was going to be hired on full time and that he would be leaving for the academy in August – a mere few months away. In the meantime he would be putting in his training time. It was all real now. Everything we had waited for and everything we had ultimately wanted was coming our way. Our prayers were answered in an untimely (to us) fashion but they were answered, nonetheless. I was now staring down the tunnel of being married to a police officer; no longer "for the season" but now for an entire season of our lives. It felt like a total overhaul of everywhere I thought our lives together were going. It was overwhelming but also blissful to know that Josh was living up to his potential that I always knew he had.

He's been officially sworn in and now we are just waiting. It's a few weeks until he is supposed to go to the academy, where he will leave for three months. We have five kids, eight and under right now, but it won't be the first time I've been left alone with small children. So many things have conditioned me for this and I realize that I will complain, and I will feel neglected. I will be sad and I will have to work through it but if Josh can suck it up and do his job, so can I. I was made for this, the same as him.

Now I'm married to a cop. I don't really understand how it happened. There are so many challenges and so many aspects of it that I didn't even fathom before. I still have a mini-panic attack when I hear sirens and see the police cars speeding through town with lights blazing. I still get that deep gut wrenching feeling when I schedule any family event, because I have learned that he won't be there. I know he is going to come home needing emotional support, he's going to be full of testosterone and probably argumentative, and he's going to be exhausted. He is changing into someone stronger, smarter, and more dependable than ever before. He's already been Tasered. He's already been pepper sprayed. He's qualified with his weapon (twice!) and been taught how to shine his shoes. It's the tip of the iceberg that no one can really fully grasp until they are in the midst of it. And we are just getting started, when I think about it. I never thought I would swoon when I heard him over the radio, and when he comes home in his uniform. I never imagined how I would worry about him constantly or that the job would be never-ending. He doesn't always come home at the end of the day just because his shift ends at 5 p.m. Ask any police wife – there is no such thing as a real timely shift. He's on pins and needles constantly because there is really only a matter of time before he is called out, even if it is his day off. There is no way to describe what it feels like, lying in bed in the middle of the night when a phone call comes in and your husband jumps out of bed and starts getting dressed. The further in we go the more I "get it." This is why there are entire communities of wives of LEOs. Those on the outside won't understand most of what it's like living from one breath to the next. The toll it takes on your family when your husband's career has to engulf everything in your lives. It's tough. It's harrowing. It's consistently inconsistent. In all honesty though, I wouldn't trade it for the world. I'm overtly proud to say I'm married to a cop. -Abby Huskey

This life is hard and challenging and is going to change you in a lot of ways. It will definitely alter your perception of the things and people around you at times. There is no way to prevent this life causing change in both of you. Some days are going to be harder than others. While there are many ways   to learn how to cope and deal with the stresses of this job so that we can be ready to support them,   none have seemed to work as well for me as prayer, and a massive   amount of it, along with time spent in the

Word to remind me that he has a greater source of protection over him. On my hardest days, because my faith has always been my anchor, it's what I turned to. If I didn't know how in the world I was supposed to reach him, to make him open up to me again, to let me in, I hit my knees and covered him in prayer. They are surrounded by darkness as they make arrests, serve warrants, do drug busts, etc., and I felt it was my responsibility to keep him lifted up even if he wasn't doing it himself. While you may not relate exactly to that, as so many have said, it all comes down to our love for him, for our hero, and the commitment that we made however many years ago. We promised that we were all in, no matter what it took, partners for life.

What words come to mind when I think of being a blue line wife?
<u>Proud</u>: *that the man I love more than life suits up every shift to go protect and serve while putting himself at risk in some shape or form of not making it home to us*
<u>Humbled</u>: *by how the men and women in blue can do so much and risk so much for very little respect in return many times.*
<u>Support</u>: *through the good and the bad days at work, I not only stay by his side, but on his side as well. I may not go out there with him, but we are still a team and I try to be his steady rock at home.*
<u>Flexible</u>: *to make it in this world of adversity, it's key to roll with the punches, figure out days you're on your own and when he's going to be home and know things can change at any time.*
: for one with communication knowing there are things he may not want to talk about at least right away. Also, the wait for his arrival back home, the garage door, front door, the sweet, sweet sound of velcro.

It would be easy for any cop wife to use words like frustrating, lonely, resentment, scary, or hard. At times, all of those things are true, but that's the case with anything. Instead it's what you make of it. From the beginning, before I knew what we were getting into, I vowed to stick by him and support him through every move and I will continue to do so. It's a scary, crazy world out there and some days I want to hold on to him for just a few more seconds and some days I don't want him to walk out that door at all. It's his calling though and I have to trust God to protect and guide him. If all I did was focus on the negative aspects this world has brought from time to time, I'd never fully appreciate the greatness of it for all of time....being proud, humbled, supportive, flexible, patient and more to his courage, hard work, strength, compassion... his calling. -Lacey

This day and age far too many people don't actually understand what a commitment truly means. They surely do not understand that "until death do we part" line! This life puts our vows to the test, often! If you are coming in reading this book as a glimpse into what your life would be like if you continue to pursue it with the guy you have been seeing, understand what this really means. None of this is shared to put a negative light on what being a cop wife means because we love this life. It is hard. Harder than we ever understood before we began walking it hand in hand with him. There has to be a deep foundation of love, commitment, loyalty, and friendship to make this work. You have to be ready to be his partner in every sense of the word. If you are, this will be the greatest adventure yet!

While it is important to understand the chaotic schedules, the mood changes, knowing that this life will have a huge impact on both of you, that is not the only factor we have to understand. Not only when we first get married to our hero, but every day after, we have to be prepared for a knock at the door, or a phone call, to tell us that he is down. It is something we have had to witness far too many times, in support of another officer's wife and family. It is heartbreaking and gut wrenching, and yet those wives have suffered through their greatest nightmares with such grace, even when their whole world is falling apart.

5 End of Watch

There is something about hearing the last call over the radio, the bagpipes playing, the 21 gun salute, that absolutely breaks your heart into a million tiny pieces for the LEOW who is having to say goodbye to her hero, her partner. She will never get the chance to see her husband come home safely from another shift. It is the call, the knock on the door, that we all know is a possibility, yet we pray that we are never ones to experience it.

However, there have been many women that have had to walk that road. They have gotten that knock on the door, where in a mere moment, their heart is shattered and their world stops as they have known it. Their hero gave the ultimate sacrifice in the line of duty. These officers love their job, they are passionate about what they do, and they all know the dangers that are present with their job, and yet they continue to put on the uniform and go out and continue working to make a difference. It has gotten even more dangerous as more people hate police officers simply because they wear the badge and these people are willing to hurt and kill officers because of it.

Who was Brian Jones? First off, he was the best father any child could ask for. He was the best

*husband any woman could ask for. He was the best
police officer any department could ask for. I was 16
years old when he walked into my father's church. He
was a 21-year-old Sailor in the United States Navy. I
had never heard of him, never even spoke to him, but I
knew that he would be my husband.*

*We got married when I was 18 years old and had
our first child the next year. Brian always wanted to be
a police officer, so he got out of the Navy and joined the
Norfolk police department. It was then that we had our
other two children. Brian loved his job and the
wonderful community he worked in! He served on the
Norfolk police department for five and a half years
before a crazy gunmen took him away.*

*As a police wife we know that it can happen but we
don't ever really think that it will. I will never forget that
night May 30, 2014. The way he bled on me at the
hospital even though he was already dead. I'll never
forget having to come home and wake our children up to
tell them. I'll never forget the pain that I have felt over
the last almost four years. I love Brian Jones more than
life and I can honestly say we had a fairytale marriage
for none and a half years. If there is anything I can say
to any police family it is to cherish every second. Let
the small things go. Love with everything in you. Never
let him go to work angry. Forgive often, because you
never know when it's the last chance, I will always love
and miss you Brian Jones. You gave me the best
chapter 1 a girl could ever ask for. -Rebekah*

This is every wife's nightmare. It is something that
we have all thought about, worried about, and prayed
over. Not many occupations hand out "death packets"
to their employees but that is exactly what each police
officer brings home to go over. This packet includes
information for us to fill out together that explains
exactly what he would want at his funeral, who would

we like to make the notification if he does die in the line of duty, etc. Who do we want to show up and tell us that our husband is gone? It is hard just thinking about it; however, some have already walked this awful road.

The Call. The call that in the back of your mind you know you may get but try not to think too much about or it will drive you crazy. It's the call that any LEO spouse dreads. I got that call at work on March 31, 2016. The call that my husband had been involved in an incident and that someone with VSP was on their way to my work to take me to MCV to see my husband. It was the longest car ride of my life, even with lights and sirens. When I arrived at the hospital and was taken into a conference room instead of a hospital room to see my husband, I knew they were going to tell me my worst nightmare had come true. My husband had been shot and killed. And my whole world was forever changed in a blink of an eye.

At 27, I was a widow. I lost my husband and best friend of 16 years. My 14 year old son and 11 year old daughter lost their father. How exactly do you tell your children that they will never see their dad again? How do you tell them that everything they once knew has been ripped from them? Having to tell them that their dad had been shot and killed at work was one of the hardest things I've ever had to do in my life. Ever. Then there's the phone calls to family and friends to tell them the news. I wanted to tell as many people as possible so that they heard it from me and not on the news. I don't know how I did it but I mustered up the strength to make the calls. My adrenaline took over.

It's been fifteen months now since my husband was killed in the line of duty. I am proud of how far I have come since that day. I am blessed with an amazing support system. People still talk about my husband which is so important to me. He will forever be

*a part of my life. I love talking about him. I tell people he
was my Chapter One in my life, and I had an amazing
Chapter One.*

*I was loved unconditionally by an incredible man
who blessed me with two beautiful children. Moving
forward, it is important for me to continue spreading my
husband's legacy. He was a man of honor and integrity
and it has become my mission to make sure that he is
not forgotten. My journey hasn't been an easy one, but I
choose to be happy, humble and kind. This tragedy has
reminded me that life is too short. So I make the most of
each and every day. I choose to live. I choose to be
better than I was the day before and I choose to be a
light in this world. It's what my husband would want
me to do.*
~Michelle Dermyer

As a group, as a sisterhood of LEOWs, we have a
bond that really can't be explained to anyone else.
They just don't understand because they don't
understand our life. While we do all have in the back
of our minds, questions and nagging fears about our
husbands' and their safety, we wonder if we are next
to hear the knock on the door, or get the call to tell us
that our nightmare is starting. However, if one of our
sister's get that call, we immediately jump in to see
how we can help. We will not allow her to have to walk
that nightmare on her own. When an officer is killed in
the line of duty, even if it's one you didn't know
personally, and they weren't from your department or
even your state, it still affects you. These women have
shown us incredible strength and determination in the
face of losing their hero and best friend. They have
shown us what grace looks like, as well as sacrifice as
they continue to put their kids first, no matter what,
even in the face of their overwhelming grief.

I think as a police wife, you always prepare yourself for that knock on the door, or the call that your officer is down. You never seem to prepare yourself to have to watch your husband be in so much pain and nothing can be done. October 16, 2014 I will forever remember the ER doctor's words. "He needs to be taken up to ICU immediately. He is in liver and kidney failure and we aren't sure yet what is going on".

At that moment I could feel my whole entire life being turned upside down. What we thought was the flu and a quick ER visit with meds and rest, turned into four days of me watching my strong husband be in so much pain, struggle to breathe, and slowly die from a bacterial infection that we had no answers on how he contracted this. October 20, 2014, I woke up as a 34 year old wife and mom to a 5 year old, to only go to bed that night as a 34 year old widow with a five year old little girl. My whole entire life was flipped and thrown in turmoil and I was left to pick up the pieces to try and repair our lives. There was just one big piece missing from our puzzle and that was my husband.

In three years I have learned a lot. I have survived with my faith, God, my daughter, family, friends and blue family. I have learned I will never be able to please or make everyone happy. I will forever be judged how I choose to live after my loss. I learned to stop letting others tell me how to grieve, and live. People ask me how I do it, and the answer is, I wasn't given an option. I just have to. I have a little girl that depends on me, and is my complete and true happiness. If it wasn't for Audrey I honestly think I would have died along with my husband. I cope with humor, sarcasm, prayers, and living my life. We have amazing family, friends, and blue family and I know deep down inside my husband would be damn proud of the decisions I've had to make and one day we will be reunited.

My life will forever be in two parts. With my husband, and after my husband. Johnnie Jones, I love you, I miss you more than anything, and I thank you for showing me unconditional love everyday of your life. Thank you for making me a mother to rambunctious, sassy, strong willed kid. Thank you for making me the woman that I am. Northeast PD EOW 10/20/2014 Badge number 421 -April

Obviously, none of us know what tomorrow is going to bring. We aren't promised a specific amount of time with anyone and we all know this. These heartbreaking stories from wives that have lost their husbands on duty simply reiterate that fact. My question to you is, how is this going to change how you treat your marriage and your hero? I understand, we all have days that we are at the end of our rope, and he has pushed us to our limit. However, that is not a good enough reason to stay angry with him or allow him to be angry with you. Especially, if he is about to leave for another shift. You do not want the lifelong regret of knowing the last thing you did with your spouse was to fight with him. That doesn't mean you have to let him slide with everything by any means, but it does mean you need to pick your battles and to let go of the petty stuff that 10 years from now, not only isn't going to matter, but you aren't even going to remember. You need to make a commitment to yourself, that no matter what, you will always let him know that you love him before he walks out of your front door.

On a typical Wednesday morning, on June 24, 2015, Chris and I were getting ready for work. Chris gave his children (ages 4 and 7) a kiss goodbye as he was leaving. He then gave me a kiss, as we all told him that we loved him and to be safe. After dropping the kids off to summer camp, I started my day at the office in a meeting. A friend texted me asking if everything was ok with Chris, as she heard someone was hurt. I began texting Chris asking him to "please be ok" but he never replied. My boss came to the meeting and asked that I go to his office as he needed to talk to me. As I entered his office I turned around to see the Chief of Police standing before me. That is when my nightmare began, that is when I was told that the love of my life was killed.

Chris was a Sergeant in the Criminal Investigations Unit (CIU). For the past 10 months I didn't worry about Chris as he mainly worked in the office. This was the first time in the 14 years of us being together that he worked day shift. Chris and I met in the United States Air Force. Chris continued his military service up until the day he was taken from us.

Chris was a selfless man who served his country as well as his community. As a family, we celebrated holidays and birthdays on days Chris was off. As a police wife you have to be flexible, understanding, and you have to learn that very few will understand the sacrifices we make when we are left alone with the kids night after night. You see, police officers don't just bleed blue, the whole family bleeds blue. It is hard, yet we are so proud of our officers so we take each day in stride and celebrate the moments we have together.

On that heart-wrenching day, in my boss' office, all I could think of, is how do I see Chris, I need to go to him! The Chief drove me to the hospital where the halls were lined with medical staff, police officers, and firefighters. It was as if I was on a cloud. I could not feel my feet. I couldn't hear the words people spoke to me. As I walked into the hospital room where my husband laid there, lifeless, all I could do was cry, hold his hand, kiss him, and tell him how much I loved him. Our family surrounded his body trying to understand how this could happen! You see, a suspect evaded a patrol officer that morning. This officer called for backup. Chris immediately got up from his office chair and went in his undercover car to help. Chris found the suspect. As he attempted to detain him, the suspect fought him, jumped into my husband's vehicle and proceeded to run him over and never looked back. That man was found guilty for murder and sentenced to life in prison in November 2017.

For many reasons, I will never forget that day. Some things are blurry and some things are very clear. I remember every detail when I told my children their Daddy would not be coming home. My children came in the house after being on a field trip that day. My daughter ran up to me telling me she had had "the best day ever" because she finally passed her swim test! In that moment, I had to then break their hearts by telling them their Daddy won't be coming home. I told them he was now with Jesus in heaven.

My daughter screamed at me and said, "Are you telling me I don't have a Daddy anymore"? My heart *stopped. I tell you this to now tell you it has been two and a half years and we are fighters...we are survivors! My daughter (ten years old) is in the 4th grade. She is so loving and honest, she is protective of her brother and I, and she loves school! My son (six years old) is in Kindergarten. He is affectionate and free-spirited and keeps us on our toes! He loves school and loves making friends. My children and I have learned to lean into God and to count our blessings. There is not a day that goes by that we don't miss him. But we continue to honor Chris by living, by telling stories about him and we started the Chris Kelley Foundation so no one will ever forget his ultimate sacrifice. Life is hard but we are forever grateful for the years we had with Chris and for the support we have been given from our blue family, our community, and the support the ladies from Cop Wives Headquarters have given me.*

Michele Kelley (Surviving Spouse of Detective Sergeant Chris Kelley of Hutto PD)

There are no words to describe what it feels like for a wife to get the call that her husband has been killed in the line of duty. There are so many emotions and things that run through their head. These same emotions run through the blue family when there is an officer killed in the line of duty. It cannot be said enough that when a brother or sister in blue is killed in the line of duty it affects all of us on some level. Your heart breaks for the family, you get angry because a blue life was lost and you get a little closer to your own spouse because it could be him or her at any time.

One thing that makes the blue family even more

amazing is how we come together for each other, especially in a time of need. When one of us hurts, we all hurt. We wrap our love and support around the spouses, their kids and their families. We make sure they have what they need. It is a testament to what our blue family is about.

In the summer of 1999, I got my first job in a busy department store. I was folding clothes when a tall, blue eyed, handsome man walked past me. I didn't really believe in love at first sight, until that day. I knew right then and there that he was the one. I told a friend that I was going to marry that man someday. She laughed at me thinking I was a little crazy, since I didn't even know him; however, I still had to find out. So smitten by him, I didn't care what my future held, as long as it was with him. He made my heart beat fast, gave me butterflies in my stomach and made me smile without saying anything at all. That day, I found out that he worked as a loss prevention associate in the same department store and he was looking for a possible suspect when I noticed him. So, of course I had to get to know him.

We soon went on our first date and my dream had come true. We were young but so in love. He was working his way through college to get his criminal justice degree. As we dated, I continued to fall in love with him and began to really hate the thought of him becoming a police officer. Although, I was so proud of him, I also hated the thought of losing him in such a dangerous job. We had several conversations about why he wanted to become a police officer. One day he finally laid it out on the line. He had wanted to become a police officer since he was 2 years old. It wasn't likely that he would change his mind. He knew it was his calling. With a history of a grandfather and great grandfather that proudly wore a badge, he knew it was in his blood. He couldn't wait to begin his journey and he would do it with or without me if he had to. He hoped that I would find a way to support him but I needed to decide.

Then he became a confidential informant for a department that was going to put him through the police academy. That is when it got real! No gun, no one with him, just him, in his truck, buying drugs in order for the cops to make an arrest. Could I live this life every day? I waited by the phone and couldn't wait to hear his voice again. It never got easier and I wondered, was this really my future? As I sat in my room worried sick, I prayed and hoped that he would be ok on a late night run. I realized that day, it didn't matter what he did. He would have a divine day like the rest of us. Whether he was a cop, a cook or a computer whiz, he would be taken from this world and there was nothing that I could do to stop it. I had to have a little denial but a whole lot of faith.

He graduated in May of 2002 from the police academy and we married later that month. The very next week after our honeymoon, he was to report for his first week on duty. We quickly adjusted to a life with him working the night shift. Although, I found peace with having him become a police officer, I began building up a wall of protection for my heart. As a cop's wife, I realized a chief, an officer or a Chaplin could show up at my door someday. Although it wasn't right, I found myself trying to be ready for something like that.

He stayed on the night shift for several years but quickly became part of the swat team and then a Sergeant of patrol. I was extremely proud of him and he did me the favor by keeping most stories to himself. Once he walked into our door, he rarely wanted to talk about work. He had already written his reports about his day and talked to other officers. He didn't want to rehash most things again. However, I knew something was wrong when he did want to talk about work because I knew he needed someone to talk to. After horrible accidents, seeing countless dead bodies or horrible situations with children, he would spare me as many details as he could but I could tell it was haunting him.

Most people will live their whole life without seeing even half of what a LEO sees in a year. He was learning how to deal/process some really horrific events. After a few years on patrol he became a CID Sergeant. I ignorantly told myself this would be better. He would spend most of his days behind a desk. Although that was true for a while, it was then that he had his first major injury on the job. He always promised me that he would call or text after a bad situation. He wanted to make sure I didn't get the news from a news report or anyone else. As long as he was breathing and alive, he would be the one to tell me. As he was getting checked into a hospital, he called to tell me where he was and that he was ok; however, I should come. While chasing a suspect he shredded his ACL and pretty much blew out his entire right knee. Surgery was necessary but I got to take him home with me that night. I was extremely thankful he was ok and alive. I still stuck with my little bit of denial and a whole lot of faith. That of course wasn't the end of his journey though. We had many more close calls.

He had his first standoff that resulted in a death the night before I gave birth to our first born. He got caught in cross fire during a shootout and heard bullets missing his head within inches. The Lord has protected him through much. After each incident, I found myself clinging closer to him, holding him tighter and thanking God that he gave me another day with him. Still I didn't lose my faith but I may have gained a little more denial. I knew I couldn't ask him to stop. I was proud of him. He had accomplished so much in a relatively short amount of time.

After about 10 years, and a department move, I noticed that more and more people would call/text me when they saw a bunch of cop's with lights and sirens going in one direction. I'd say a quick prayer but wouldn't get panicked. I knew that didn't always mean an officer was down or that they were in immediate danger. I would just wait for his text or call. Sometimes when it felt like it had been too long, I'd send the first text to make sure he was ok. I am very thankful to say, I always received an "I'm ok". I knew I could get details later but as long as he was ok, that is all I needed to know.

The summer of 2015, things changed. For 13 years, I heard him strap on that heavy vest and belt, put his radio in its holster, grab a hand full of keys and walk towards me with those clunky boots to say goodbye. He'd kiss me, we exchange our "I love you's" and I'd tell him to be safe. I always believed he and his buddies would be. I knew they'd come home. After all, they did for years, until June 24, 2015. It didn't feel like a different kind of day but it marked a change in our lives forever. That morning we carried on with our regular routine but a close friend texted me to see what was going on, as she saw a bunch of cops flying by. I told her, I didn't know but I was sure it was fine. I wasn't going to worry; I believed in our guys and my faith was bigger than that. I went about with my business and then got a text, "I'm ok". Part of me was relieved but I had faith and I knew everything was ok until I got his call. I couldn't understand him and finally, I made out his buddy's name. I was crushed. I knew it was bad and he couldn't talk. He promised to call me later. I literally dropped to the floor. I began begging God to save our friend's soul. I didn't know how bad it was but I knew God did. I asked God to wrap his arms around him and to help the first responders to work quickly. I began to get angry and told God, "do not take that soul"! I begged Him to keep him here for his wife and babies. I repeated my prayer over and over.

Less than a half hour later, we got the dread call. Our nightmare was true. The nightmare we knew could always happen but surely not to one of our guys, right? This would never happen in our town but we couldn't be in denial anymore. We were facing our nightmare. Feeling completely helpless and broken, I didn't know what to do. I wanted to hold his wife, babies and feeling selfish, I desperately wanted to hold my husband too. I realized it could have been him and it could be him one day. Fear came over me but I tried not to focus on that. All I was thinking about was, "where was I supposed to go, what was I supposed to do?"

This couldn't be real. I was angry, I was panicked, I was scared and I was sobbing.

This began a new journey of a very painful and broken road, as we mourned the loss of our friend and our brother. However, we found out what it meant to be part of a blue family. We cried together, we hugged one another tightly and we felt each other's pain. It was our small beauty among the deep ashes. No one will understand your fear and hurt like a blue family member. We felt a little peace just being together. Even in our pain, what hurt the most was how broken we were for the family. The only thing we knew to do was overwhelm them with our love and support. We all wanted to find a way to take the hurt away but it was inevitable. He was gone and we will forever be different. The loss of a blue family member will change you. You will remember how dangerous this job is, like the first day they pinned on that badge and walked out that door. It will remind you that life is short and you should hug your loved ones a little tighter for a little longer. It will bring fear and it will bring pain. You will lose sight of hope for a little while and maybe even be angry with God. However, it will break walls and you will learn how to really love and be loved by people you don't even know. Look for the beauty among the ashes because the pain will overwhelm you.

Somehow we will find our way back to little bit of denial and a whole lot of faith but we will never be the same. Our brother is gone but will never be forgotten. Only those that have a true calling will survive the loss of his brother. He will put that badge on with pride and do it for a new reason, for his brother. Otherwise, it was all in vain. Over time, I've learned that most LEO's

don't talk about their work for a reason. They are
trying to spare your heart and mind. This wasn't their
first time to fight the pain of this evil world and it won't
be their last. Be there, ready to listen and to hold tight.
They are going to need someone strong to stand by
them through it all.

We will always celebrate the lives and remember
the sacrifices that these officers have made. We will
never forget them. We will forever stand beside their
spouses and family.

6 Wife to Wife

This life is amazing, chaotic, stressful, scary, exhilarating, and everything in between. There is no other life quite like it and unless someone is living it, or has lived it, they can't truly understand what we deal with on a daily basis. I think we can all agree that we have had some crazy, stupid, random, hilarious stuff come up as a cop's wife. Whether it's the call they get and the text that follows, what piece of equipment he leaves at home on accident, and many others. So here are some funny cop wives stories and lots of advice, just for you, from other law enforcement wives!

My first encounter with my husband's sergeant as a new LEOW was a learning experience. I came to the police department to return a casserole dish to the wife of one of the other officers. Sergeant came around the corner and noticed the dish before he even introduced himself. Looking like a kid at Christmas, "What's in the dish?" he asked. I shrugged my shoulders, "Oh, it's empty. I'm just bringing it back." He says, "Don't you know, you never bring empty casserole dishes into a police department." Boom. First lesson as a police wife. Thanks sergeant. ~ Amy T.

As the wife of a fairly new (less than 2 years active

duty) police officer, I am still very much in the learning process of our new life we call the LEO Life. My husband made a complete 180 career change; it came at a pretty perfect time in our life and marriage, mid-twenties, no children yet, great time for a change. But I will tell you, it isn't easy or perfect all the time. There has been doubt, disappointment, tears, lonely nights, stress, and misunderstandings; but there's also been an increase of faith, encouragement, love, honor, LEO family, new opportunities, and appreciation. So from the super serious, to the super comical, I'll share the best tips I can, for things you can expect from being a LEOW:

- *Learn to be flexible – meal times, holidays, date nights, future plans – repeat after me, your new mantra is "be flexible"!*
- *Planning ahead requires some effort – oftentimes planning far in advance is best, so you ensure your husband/partner can ask off in plenty of time; other times, mandatory OT will come up two weeks before he's required to work and your advanced planning efforts are thwarted. It's a balancing act!*
- *He will probably have to work holidays (especially early on in his career). Try to make the holiday special in your own way or start your own holiday tradition by celebrating the day before or the day after the actual holiday – this way he (and your family) doesn't have to miss out!*
- *Get used to having conversations over/above his radio while he's on duty; I've learned to wait until the dialogue on the radio is over so we can talk! And don't freak out when he cuts you off to say, "Gotta go, call you back".*
- *Never underestimate the power of a warrant arrest to ruin your plans. (Or drunk driver, or*

domestic, or (insert your experience here).

- *Make time for dates.*
- *Communication is key – leave love notes around the house for him to find, send encouraging texts throughout his shift, and find time to really talk.*
- *Go on a Ride-Along with him – it will help you understand (and appreciate) his job so much better and you'll also learn what keeps him so busy on his shift!*
- *Sometimes he will want to talk about his shift, sometimes he won't. Discuss this together and how you will handle this particular communication before you get there – trust me it will help you both tremendously in the long run.*
- *Limit watching/reading the news and reading negative stories about police officers – you'll want to lash out at complete strangers (or, unfortunately, misunderstood friends/family), and it could even scare you unnecessarily.*
- *Be very wary of what you share about his profession (including photos) on social media – you can never be too careful! I want to show the whole world how proud I am of my man in uniform, but it's much safer not to.*
- *Try not to berate him for getting late home from work – more than likely, he had a really rough shift and getting home two hours later than expected doesn't make him any happier than it does you.*
- *You'll learn not to ask 'how his day was' – he will share what he needs, when he needs.*
- *He is never really off duty.*
- *Be supportive, even if you don't always want to be.*
- *Find your own hobbies to do while he's on shift – think Pinterest! I catch up on my favorite TV shows, do laundry, read a good book, take a*

bubble bath, etc.

- *Get a subscription to Spotify or XM Radio for his unit – good tunes can help a 12-hour grave shift go by a little quicker!*
- *Find little ways to lift his spirits; men like surprises too! A simple text message while he's on shift, tickets to a game or movie, special lunch or fresh cookies delivered to him at work, etc., makes all the difference.*
- *Show your support and show it often!*
- *Make friends with fellow police wives and families – no one will understand your life better than they do!*
- *Get involved with your police department happenings if you can – join the auxiliary, or start one to support your hubby, fellow officers, and department!*
- *Always kiss him goodbye, always say 'I love you' before he leaves for work – No. Matter. What.*
- *Pray – I can't stress how having faith in God, reading devotionals, and praying together has strengthened our marriage, especially after my husband became a LEO.*
- *Don't put stock in the statistics – statistics regarding LEO's and their spouses are dismally depressing and do not need to be your story – so we choose to ignore them and create our own life!*
- *Recognize that he may need help and advice about the job that you may not be able to help with; encourage him to talk to his supervisor, another 'brother' in the department, or even professional counseling that may be offered through your department.*
- *Being a LEOW means a mutual respect for the job and lifestyle – we learn to see the bigger picture. –M.S.*

So we were engaged at the time, still having to do the long distance deal, which wasn't as awful as it could have been. I would come up on the weekends, and ride along with him usually at least part of one night that he was working. Well, that night I just didn't feel like riding around for very long, so went back to his apartment since he wasn't going to be there anyway. He had said he would come by on his break when he dropped me off.

It wasn't an hour later that he texted and said they were slammed and that he would never make it by, but he would see me tomorrow. I said that it was no big deal and watched a little tv and then decided to take a shower. So I had taken my gun into the bathroom with me and set it on the back of the toilet, just in case, and got in the shower.

Probably 10 minutes later, as I was still in the shower, all of a sudden all of the lights go out. My heart instantly sinks thinking that someone has broken in. So my hand goes immediately to my gun, when all of a sudden I hear "BABY! Wait, it's just me! Sorry!" I. Could. Have. Killed. Him in that instant. I flipped out, telling him how he was close to being shot because I was not going to have some psychopath come and take me! I told him those newspaper articles reading "Deputy Shot By Fiancé When He Pranks Her" would have been terrible! So that night we made a rule between the two of us that we were never allowed to scare or prank the other like that again because we both kept ourselves armed most of the time! Problem solved!
-Jess

So, my first wife experience happened one weekend while the kiddo was staying at the grandparents. We had a romantic dinner and spent alone time together. We got awoken to the sound of breaking glass about 2am. Let's preface this with the fact that we lived in a rough area. So up jumps hubby out of bed grabbing his duty weapon and starts clearing the house, room by room, like a Naked Greek God. Once he checked all windows and doors he came back to say nothing was amiss, but we both knew the sound came from inside our house. I was still scared, but I went to the restroom, and there I found that one of our glass shelves had broken and fallen on the floor. We had left a candle lit and the heat broke the glass. OOPS! I still laugh to this day when I think of him jumping into action naked as a newborn baby. -Anonymous

It can be comical sometimes how we automatically assume that any noise means something bad. Usually, we get a pretty good laugh out of it when we find what the noise really was. Not only are these things laughable but the stories that some of our LEO's come home to tell us make us laugh just as hard. Here are a few stories of some of these instances that will never be forgotten:

So one night, I get a text from my husband "got into a fight, but I'm ok". He normally clarifies so I know whether to little panic or big panic. Shortly after, he calls me and says "you'll never believe this" and I would have 100% thought he made it up, if the pepper spray outline of a face wasn't still on his back glass when   he   arrived   home   that   night.

My husband arrived at a local grocery store, where theft prevention had two guys waiting for him due to stealing some deli items. They of course swear they didn't do it. "You're literally still eating the chicken they have you on video stealing," my husband responded, "so go ahead and put that down." Now the theft prevention office is about the size of a sneeze. How they even got three people in it to begin with is impressive. One of the suspects throws his drumstick down like a girl pulling out her earrings before a brawl, rears back and goes for my husband. They fight all through the tiny little office, all while his partner sits on the couch, periodically moving out of the way of their tussling.

My husband ends up pepper spraying the belligerent suspect and finally gets him in cuffs. When they get out to the car, he gets a little wild again and ends up pushed up against the back glass and I kid you not you could see a smashed up cheek, nose, and lips all outlined in red....all over some fried chicken! – Dani

-The hubby came home 4 hours early one night while on night shift, without letting me know. He was met at the door by me carrying a gun! We live out in the country and had no close neighbors at the time. If you come in my door after I lock it for the night, you are going to be met with a gun! Our bedroom door is between the front and back doors so you can't get in without me knowing. He learned that the hard way! -Tina

-My husband forgot his radio on the day the President came to town for a funeral after the church shooting here in Charleston, SC. To get where he worked, I had to cross the path the President traveled on. Now, for those that don't know, once the President lands, they shut down the entire route until he gets to his destination. It's the safest and fastest way to move him, but it does cause a backup for anyone who would need to cross the path. My hubby called and said he forgot his radio and the first thing I said was "So?". Of course, I knew I would have to take it to him. The President was already at the funeral and talking so I found a local radio station playing him speaking live and I flew (within reason) to where the hubs was. I opened the window and threw the radio at him and started back home praying I'd make it back across the path before they wanted to move the President back to the air base. I made it, but I remember listening to the radio and thinking for the first time ever, "Please don't stop talking

Mr. President!" Police wives, whether it's a gun, radio, phone, body cam, etc., we are going to drop everything and take it in for our husbands! Even if the President of the United States is in our way! -Misty

-My husband and I moved into a brand new house on a street with only a few houses. It was our second night in the house and we just got into bed for the night. All of a sudden, clear as day you would have thought someone just broke into our house through a window. It was loud and sounded like glass breaking or shattering. We jump out of the bed, and of course the hubby grabs his gun and tells me to stay upstairs and call 911 if something happens. He goes and clear every room of our house and the basement and he yells "ALL CLEAR!!". So I come downstairs. All of a sudden we hear the crashing noise again. He opens the front door and there is my Valentine's Day door decoration bashing against my glass front door when the wind picked up. OOPS!! I had to take it down, but never felt so safe in my entire life. -Cathy

-I was still working EMS and I had come home late, probably 2300. The husband was still part time LEO and working as a CSM at a grocery store. He had fallen asleep on the couch waiting for me to come home and I'm not a quiet person, so I woke him up while unlocking the door. I was halfway through the door when he jumped off the couch and drew his Glock that was on the coffee table, obviously this is before we had kids, and aimed at me while yelling some half asleep mumbo jumbo and I quickly jumped backwards out the door and slammed it. He came over and sheepishly opened the door and said, "Sorry baby!" I have never let him forget this! -Kazandra

-The hubby always checks his equipment before work. In order to check his taser, he removes the cartridge

before pulling the trigger. One night he was getting ready to leave and doing his nightly check. I was laying on the couch reading on my phone until I saw the red laser beam on my chest. I looked up and smiled knowing he was trying to get my attention. I smiled and told him that he wouldn't dare. (He joked with my daughter a lot that he was going to tase Mama when I wasn't paying attention.) He smiled back, put the cartridge back on the taser, and I went back to my phone. I heard the noise of the taser, and at the same time he screamed! (He had removed the cartridge again without me seeing it.) I was so convinced that he had tased me that I was shaking and I peed my pants! He and my daughter were in the kitchen laughing so hard! When I realized that I had not in fact been tased, I had no choice but to laugh too! The power of suggestion is a powerful thing! He did the same thing a few months later with inert OC spray canister they use for training. "Hey babe, I'm so pissed! My OC spray won't work!" As he proceeds to push down on the top to prove it doesn't and it sprays me right in the face! I was on my feet that time in the laundry room, he's lucky that he is faster than me! -Kimberly

-When I first dated my husband I went on a ride along, my very first one. We were on a call for DV and they ended up arresting the husband. He was in the back of the cruiser yelling and cussing. While we were transporting him to the jail, I kept hearing trickling sounds. I turn around to see and this man has his penis out and is peeing everywhere in the backseat. I could not believe it! I was so thankful that the windows were closed! -Bethany

-While on a ride along with my husband, we stopped to assist two drunk men that had passed out at a bus stop bench. Upon my husband securing the scene, I got out of the car and was standing off to the side asking my

husband questions about this particular call, and one of the men became combative with me. Calling me every name in the book and threatening to do some really bad things to me. So, me being me, I start talking crap back because my husband is dealing with the other drunk, and I think he can't hear me, so as I'm ripping drunko a new one about how I wasn't at all afraid of the things he was threatening to do to me, my husband's SGT walked up behind me and he heard it all! Luckily, we had hung out a few times and he knew how I was. He just laughed and told the man he shouldn't talk to females like that and then put him in the back of the ambulance for his free ride to detox. – Damian

So many cop wives have the bullets in the washing machine story (and their pens!) and as a LEOW for almost 30 years, I have washed and dried my share of bullets. My husband was a Bomb Technician for the State Police for several years so this story will make sense with that little bit of background information. One day I washed a load of clothes and when I was putting it all in the dryer, I found a long piece of orange plastic string (like the kind found on a weed eater). I thought it was strange that he had some in his pocket since we have a lawn service that does all of this for us. I called out to him and said, "honey why do you have weed whacker string in your clothes? I just washed clothes and found it when I was moving things to the dryer." I heard the boom of the recliner being put down in a hurry and he came walking through the kitchen and said, "What? Let me see it!" So I gave it to him and he looked at it and said, "that's not weed whacker string, that's det cord. I'll take that." And promptly took it and put it in his car. We still laugh about that one! -Michele Fowler

We all know that once on duty, always on duty. They just can't help themselves, and do not know how to turn it off. That can be quite helpful in some situations, they are always watching and scanning to make sure one of their past arrests aren't going to see and target their family, however in some instances they just can't deny the opportunity for a short adrenaline rush.

One thing about being a police wife is that no matter where you go, even in another state, your husband will always be the police. My funny story starts on a weekday that my husband and I had gone to Tuscaloosa, AL to look run some errands. Once we left from eating we took a wrong turn and ended up in downtown Tuscaloosa. As we are sitting at the red light, we hear two cars collide and look up and notice only one vehicle in the median with its bumper tore off. My husband goes into police mode and guns it, through a red light I might add, to chase after the hit-and-run driver. As he is going through the red light, we get almost t-boned by an oncoming car while I am screaming at him to stop.

We get through that safely and ask some dog walkers if the van in front of us was the one that hit the car. They said yes. So, we catch up to the van and I call 9-1-1 with the tag number and description of the vehicle because, you know, a police wife is going to give every last detail they see right?! The van started to drive in a random pattern and eventually pulls into a Taco Bell, goes through the drive-thru (without ordering) and then, after realizing he was being followed, pulls into a parking spot. Of course, my husband pulls into the parking spot right next to the hit-and-run drive with my side of the vehicle being on his driver side.

Shortly after, Tuscaloosa PD shows up. The suspect gets out, can't speak English, has no license, no insurance, and a Guatemala passport. My husband speaks to the officer for a minute while the perp is leaned against his driver door staring at me! Of course, I do the playing on my phone, pretending I don't see you thing. After my husband gets done talking with the officer, we leave and go finish our errands. So, our shopping day turned into an adrenaline rushing car chase with a hit-and-run driver, in a state that we have no jurisdiction, but my husband is the police so what can you do? -Misty

And like any good police wife, since we are married to the law, we know how crazy our heroes can get about us following traffic laws. So we all follow them to the letter, of course! That is what we will say, anyway. But what happens when we get pulled over?

My husband was working another overtime spot at work as a Deputy Sheriff. I learned very early in my marriage to make plans to do things, so I would not sit around wishing and missing my husband while he was gone. Not that I didn't miss him, I just kept myself busy with other things. I was at my sister's house, we had eaten dinner, played with my nephew and my girls, and my son and I were watching a movie with my sister. My husband and I had a son and two girls. He called and said he was on his way home and that he had gotten off earlier than anticipated. Steve loves having his family home when he gets in from a rough day of work. He loves to give all the kids and I hugs and kisses as soon as he walks in the door, of course the dogs need to get some attention from Dad too. I asked how long he would be, as we were just finishing up our movie. He told me he would be home in about 20 minutes.

We finished the movie and gathered our things. I had to put my nephew to bed because he wanted me to tuck him in. Finally, we got out the door and my husband calls to see where we are at and I told him we are on our way. I hadn't made it half way home and all of sudden I am lit up with lights. I knew I wasn't speeding, I had just looked at my speedometer. I handed my phone to the girls and told them to call Dad that I was being pulled over and had no idea why. I am finally pulled over bright lights are hitting all my mirrors, my heart is pounding, I am trying to think what I had done wrong to be pulled over. I roll down my window and place my hands on the steering wheel and look forward. All of sudden I hear a voice say license, registration and a kiss please and then a giggle. Can you say the hubby was in so much trouble when he got home? But yes, he did get his kiss and we still laugh about this until this day.-Denise

This life is a lot of things all rolled up into one lifetime of adventure. Adventures aren't always fun, they aren't always easy and it's a lot of hard work, taking time to secure your lodging, gather resources, mapping out where you want to go, and how it is you're going to get there. Then taking into account what nature may throw into the loop. That is really what being a cop wife is all about. You have to work together as a team. I understand that at times that may be the hardest thing for you to do. Because something is bothering him but you don't know what and you can't get it out of him, but be there for him anyways. You are his partner. That means supporting him when he needs it, listening if he needs to get it off of his chest and hitting him across the head with a 2X4 if he just isn't understanding! Make a plan with him, dream with him, where do yall want to be in five years, in 10 years! Then make a game plan to make it happen. Encourage each other to stick to it.

Find small ways to tell and show him that he is your hero and you do love and adore him. Leave notes in his patrol car, or lunch you pack, in the pocket of his uniform. Know that it is OK for you to get mad and frustrated at what this job has done to your husband, that it has made him more cynical and pessimistic than he was before. All of us wives have had moments we wish we could clear the negative affects this life has had on our heroes. But we can't. So we all have to be in this together. Knowing that you are never alone. That you will always have an enormous sisterhood in the blue line family, no matter what.

Find the humor and laughter in the small things. Work on letting go of the petty things that cause dumb arguments. It's just not worth it. You and your cop have something special. You both knew it when you first got together. You let go of all of your reservations about what being in this life, in this blue family would be like. You went all in for him. Your marriage is more than just the badge, however the badge does play a huge role in it. You just have to work and adjust until you find that happy medium that works for the two of you. While we all have a lot of factors in common, only you know your marriage. Only you know your hero.

I hope this has helped you in some way or maybe just made you laugh and feel more at peace knowing there are so many just like you, that have felt exactly what you have been feeling. You are not alone, and we will always have your six!

Epilogue

In closing, we hope that this book has in some small way benefited you. Maybe all you needed was to know that you most definitely are not alone in what you feel as you walk the blue line. Each day can bring emotions from one extreme to the other, pride so big your heart could burst, and then seeing red because for the fifth night in a row you have spent so much time on dinner and he comes home hours late having already eaten. It's ok. You just have to take it one day at a time. Always remember that you chose him and he chose you for a reason. This life is chaotic, but by finding yourself a good support system you can absolutely make it and do it well.

Perhaps you are one that your marriage has been rough lately or even to the point of not together in this moment, it's not too late. It is never too late as long as you have even a small desire to fight for him, to fight for each other. It's worth trying. If you have just been feeling less than worthy or confident in yourself because of kids, schedules, or whatever it may be, know that YOU. ARE. Worthy. You are the one that he wanted by his side doing this insane life together. He saw something in you, however many years ago he first stole your heart, and you were captivated by him. It's time to get back to that. To get back to each other.

That requires a crazy amount of effort and being disciplined about it. That does not mean that if you can't find hours of extra time to be together, then all hope is lost. Absolutely not! But you do have to prioritize each other, commit to at least 15 minutes of just the two of you each day. If that means getting up a little earlier, do it. If that means you climb out of bed at 2am when he is finally home and go sit in the kitchen with him, or go sit in the shower with him and just be there with him. That is where it starts.

Learn from the mistakes that we have made. Do things better than we did, don't have regrets 8 years into your marriage, knowing it could have been better than it was at that point. Remind him and yourself of the fun you two have together, the goofing off, the laughter, just being with him, even if its lying in bed and chatting about how you two met in the first place.

Remind him that he is your hero and why he is. Remind yourself that you are a badass cop wife and if you can handle this life, you can dang sure handle anything else life throws at you. This life is not for the faint of heart, for those that are willing to throw in the towel when things get a little rough. Because they will get rough, probably more times than you can count. But together, the two of you, can overcome it all. Be stronger together because of it. Learn to forgive each other, forget your anger, stop obsessing over the small stuff, realize that there is no one else in this world that gets to pick up that man's mess, or find his Under Armor shirt for the millionth time, or clean up the hair he left in the sink from shaving. Because all of those things that may drive us crazy about each other, is just something else we get to do to serve and love them.

Hopefully you have been able to see yourself throughout this book. Maybe it has shed a little light on your husband at the same time. This sisterhood that we have, walking this Thin Blue Line together, is better than any other support system out there! Go get your tribe. Each of you is amazing, strong, beautiful, and worthy. Remember that. Don't ever let this life dim any of that truth for you.

He's More

More than a badge number hanging on a wall
Heading out to call after call
More than a voice heard over the air
Backing up his brothers, he's always there
More than a car with sirens and lights
Keeping people safe, breaking up fights

He's the man I fell in love with so many years ago
With the most gorgeous smile and blue eyes that glow
Being held in those strong arms, I've always felt safe
The touch of his hand, hugs, and kisses make my day
And one of the very best days of my life
Was the day this man took me as his wife

More than a figure in the notorious hat
Having to show up where trouble and tragedy are at
More than a ticket book full of ink
Keeping people safe without having to think
More than handcuffs and a holstered gun
Protecting and serving isn't always fun

He's the father of my kids, a loving husband and Dad
There to play rough house even after his shift was bad
There's nothing like seeing him snuggle our precious child
It brings him back to us after work has been wild
Tickle games, family dates, time off is the best
Reconnecting, rejuvenating, catching up on rest

So he's more than all those details part of his career
But his courage helps him through any doubt and fear
Not everyone is cut out for this life
Either as an LEO or the wife
The evil, tragedies, rumors, crime, and hate
Just to hear him come home is the hardest wait

So he's not the same man I fell for long ago
He's changed and hardened, but our love has still grown
There will never be anyone prouder of him than his kids and his wife
We'll support him on the beat and cherish each off night
He's more to us than I could ever put in words to say
We still need him, Lord, please don't take him away

~Lacey

Afterword

Cop Wives Headquarters, also known as CWHQ, was started in 2013 with a mission to bring wives of current and former law enforcement officers together so that we could have a support system that understood what we were going through. Little did we know that what was created was so much more than that. Today, we have 340 members from all across the United States, Canada and Australia. We are no longer just a support system but we are a family.

It is our goal to support one another and support law enforcement officers in any way we can. We have done this through fundraisers over the years for different causes such as raising money for: the Kelley family, the families of the fallen officers in Dallas, TX and Baton Rouge, LA, the National Law Enforcement Memorial fund, C.O.P.S, Law Enforcement United, and many more. We feel that it is important for us to let our officers know that we care and are here for them.

We want all men and women in law enforcement to know that we appreciate all that you do. We are the Thin Blue Line and we couldn't be more proud.

Resources

There are many resources available online for police families. In the pages following you will find our copy of our "End of Watch" packet that we make available to our group members. Please feel free to use this resource to prepare your family in case of injury or death. The final page of this book will have some our group contact information that you may also use as a resource as needed.

CWHQ is, in no way, giving legal or tax advice, nor are we saying that these are the only things you will need in case of emergency. The following pages should only be used as a guide.

EOW Packet

Accounts

Company/Bank Name:

_____

Account Number:

_____

Contact:

_____

Other Information:

_____

_____

Company/Bank Name:

_____

Account Number:

_____

Contact:

_____

Other Information:

_____

_____

Company/Bank Name:

_____

Account Number:

_____

Contact:

_____

Other Information:

_____

_____

Burial Preferences

Funeral Home:

_____

Funeral Home Contact Information:

_____

_____

Preferred Law Enforcement Protocols:

_____

_____

_____

Order of Service:

_____

_____

_____

_____

Music to Play:

_____

_____

Speakers:

_____

_____

_____

Pallbearers:

_____

_____

Cemetery:

Cemetery Service to Include:

Donations to be made to:

Flowers to be sent to:

Career Achievements

Achievement:

_____

_____

When Was It Awarded:

_____

Why Was It Awarded:

_____

_____

Achievement:

_____

_____

When Was It Awarded:

_____

Why Was It Awarded:

_____

_____

Achievement:

_____

_____

When Was It Awarded:

_____

Why Was It Awarded:

_____

_____

Health Care Directive

Advance Health Care Directive

Name _____

Date _____

You have the right to give instructions about your own health care. You also have the right to name someone else to make health care decisions for you. This form also lets you write down your wishes regarding donation of organs and the designation of your primary physician. If you use this form, you may complete or change all or any part of it.

You have the right to change or revoke this advance health care directive at any time.

Part 1 — Power of Attorney for Health Care

(1.1)   DESIGNATION OF AGENT: I designate the following individual as my agent to make health care decisions for me:

Name of individual you choose as agent:

_____

Relationship

_____

Address:

_____

Telephone numbers: (Indicate home, work, cell)

_____

ALTERNATE AGENT (Optional): If I revoke my agent's authority or if my agent is not willing, able, or reasonably available to make a health care decision for me, I designate as my first alternate agent:

Name of individual you choose as alternate agent:

_____

Relationship

_____

Address:

_____

Telephone numbers: (Indicate home, work, cell)

_____

SECOND ALTERNATE AGENT (optional): If I revoke the authority of my agent and first alternate agent or if neither is willing, able, or reasonably available to make a health care decision for me, I designate as my second alternate agent:

Name of individual you choose as second alternate agent:

_____

Address:

_____

Telephone numbers: (Indicate home, work, cell)

_____

(1.2)

AGENT'S AUTHORITY: My agent is authorized to 1) make all health care decisions for me, including decisions to provide, withhold, or withdraw artificial nutrition and hydration and all other forms of health care to keep me alive, 2) to choose a particular physician or health care facility, and 3) to receive or consent to the release of medical information and records, except as I state here:

_____

_____

_____

(1.3)

WHEN AGENT'S AUTHORITY BECOMES EFFECTIVE: My agent's authority becomes effective when my primary physician determines that I am unable to make my own health care decisions unless I initial the following line. If I initial this line, my agent's authority to make health care decisions for me takes effect immediately. _____

(1.4)

AGENT'S OBLIGATION: My agent shall make health care decisions for me in accordance with this power of attorney for health care, any instructions I give in Part 2 of this form, and my other wishes to the extent known to my agent. To the extent my wishes are unknown, my agent shall make health care decisions for me in accordance with what my agent determines to be my best interest. In determining my best interest, my agent shall consider my personal values to the extent known to my agent.

(1.5)

AGENT'S POST DEATH AUTHORITY: My agent is
authorized to make anatomical gifts, authorize an autopsy,
and direct disposition of my remains, except as I state here
or in Part 3 of this form:

_____

_____

_____

(1.6)

NOMINATION OF CONSERVATOR: If a conservator of my
person needs to be appointed for me by a court, I nominate
the agent designated in this form. If that agent is not
willing, able, or reasonably available to act as conservator, I
nominate the alternate agents whom I have named. _____
(initial here)

Part 2 — Instructions for Health Care

If you fill out this part of the form, you may strike out any
wording you do not want.

(2.1)

END-OF-LIFE DECISIONS

 I direct my health care providers and others involved in my
care to provide, withhold, or withdraw treatment in
accordance with the choice I have marked below:

_____a) Choice Not To Prolong

I do not want my life to be prolonged if the likely risks and
burdens of treatment would outweigh the expected benefits,

or if I become unconscious and, to a realistic degree of medical certainty, I will not regain consciousness, or if I have an incurable and irreversible condition that will result in my death in a relatively short time.

Or

_____b) Choice To Prolong

I want my life to be prolonged as long as possible within the limits of generally accepted medical treatment standards.

(2.2)

OTHER WISHES: If you have different or more specific instructions other than those marked above, such as: what you consider a reasonable quality of life, treatments you would consider burdensome or unacceptable, write them here.

_____

_____

_____

Part 3 — Donation of Organs at Death (Optional)

(3.1)

Upon my death (mark applicable box):

_____I give any needed organs, tissues, or parts

_____I give the following organs, tissues or parts only:

_____

_____

_____

_____I do not wish to donate organs, tissues or parts.

My gift is for the following purposes (strike out any of the
following you do not want):

_____Transplant

_____Therapy

_____Research

_____Education

Part 4 — Primary Physician (Optional)

(4.1)

I designate the following physician as my primary
physician:

Name of Physician:

_____

Address:

_____

Telephone:

_____

Part 5 — Signature

(5.1)

EFFECT OF A COPY: A copy of this form has the same effect as the original.

(5.2)

SIGNATURE: Sign name: WITNESS: Sign name:

_____

_____

Date: Date:

_____

_____

(5.3)

STATEMENT OF WITNESSES: I declare under penalty of perjury under the laws of California (1) that the individual who signed or acknowledged this advance health care directive is personally known to me, or that the individual's identity was proven to me by convincing evidence (2) that the individual signed or acknowledged this advance directive in my presence (3) that the individual appears to be of sound mind and under no duress, fraud, or undue influence, (4) that I am not a person appointed as agent by this advance directive, and (5) that I am not the individual's health care provider, an employee of the individual's health care provider, the operator of a community care facility, an employee of an operator of a community care facility, the operator of a residential care facility for the elderly nor an employee of an operator of a residential care facility for the elderly.

Important Contacts

(department contact, family, friends, etc.)

Name:

_____

Phone Number:

_____

Address:

_____

Email Address:

_____

Alternate Ways to Contact:

_____

Name:

_____

Phone Number:

_____

Address:

_____

Email Address:

_____

Alternate Ways to Contact:

Insurance Policies

Medical Insurance Information:

Insurance Provider:

_____

Group Number:

_____

ID #:

_____

Plan Codes:

_____

Contact Information:

_____

_____

Additional Information:

_____

_____

Life Insurance Information

Insurance Provider:

_____

Group Number:

_____

ID #:

_____

Plan Codes:

Contact Information:

Additional Information:

Items to Have

Items that you will need to have copies of:

- birth certificates for all members of immediate family
- social security cards for all members of immediate family
- marriage certificate (numerous copies)
- death certificate (numerous copies – at least 10)
- if military, you will need discharge paperwork
- line of duty death benefit information
- police union information

Will and Testament

LAST WILL AND TESTAMENT OF

_____

[Name of Testator]

I, _____ [Name of
Testator], a resident of _____, [State], being of
sound and disposing mind and memory and over the age of
eighteen (18) years, and not being actuated by any duress,
menace, fraud, mistake, or undue influence, do hereby
make, publish and declare the following to be my Last Will
and Testament, revoking all previous will and codicils made
by me.

I. MARRIAGE AND CHILDREN

I declare that I am married to
_____, and all references
in this Will to my _____ [husband or wife] are
references to _____ [him or her].

 I have the following children:

Name: _____ Birth Date:
_____

Name: _____ Birth Date:
_____

Name: _____ Birth Date:
_____

Name: _____ Birth Date:

_____

II. EXECUTOR: I appoint my spouse

_____ as Executor of my
Last Will and Testament. If my spouse is unable or
unwilling to serve, then I appoint

_____ as alternate Executor.

My Executor shall be authorized to carry out all provisions
of this Will and pay my just debts, obligations and funeral
expenses, except mortgage notes secured by real estate, as
soon as practical.

III. SIMULTANEOUS DEATH OF SPOUSE: If my

_____ [wife or husband] shall die
simultaneously with me, I direct that I shall be deemed to
have survived my _____ [wife or husband], and
that the provisions of my Will shall be construed on such
presumption.

IV. SIMULTANEOUS DEATH OF BENEFICIARY: If any

beneficiary of this Will, other than my _____
[wife or husband], shall die within 30 days of my death or
prior to the distribution of my estate, I hereby declare that I
shall be deemed to have survived such person.

V. BEQUESTS:

I will give the persons named below, if he or she survives
me, the Property described below:

Name: _____

Address: _____

Relationship: _____

Property:

_____

Name: _____

Address: _____

Relationship: _____

Property:

Name: _____

Address: _____

Relationship: _____

Property:

If a named beneficiary to this Will predeceases me, the bequest to such person shall lapse, and the property shall pass under the other provisions of this Will. If I do not possess or own any property listed above on the date of my death, the bequest of that property shall lapse.

VI. **ALL REMAINING PROPERTY; RESIDUARY CLAUSE**: I give, devise, and bequeath all of the rest, residue, and remainder of my estate, of whatever kind and character, and wherever located, to my _____ [wife or husband], provided that my _____ [wife or husband] survives me. I make no provision for my children, knowing that, as their parent, my _____ [wife or husband] will continue to be mindful of their needs and requirements. If my _____ [wife or husband] does not survive me, then I give, devise, and bequeath all of the rest, residue, and remainder of my estate, of whatever kind and character, and wherever located, to my children per share, but if any child predeceases me, then his or her share will pass, per share, to his or her lineal descendants, natural or adopted, if any, who survive me; but if there are none, I direct that the share of any child of mine who shall have died leaving no issue shall be divided among my surviving children in equal shares.

VII. ADDITIONAL POWERS OF THE EXECUTOR: My Executor shall have the following additional powers with respect to my estate, to be exercised from time to time at my Executor's discretion without further license or order of any court.

_____

_____

VIII. OPTIONAL PROVISIONS: I have placed my initials next to the provisions below that I adopt as part of this Will. Any unmarked provision is not adopted by me and is not a part of this Will.

_____ If any beneficiary to this Will is indebted to me at the
__ time of my death, and the beneficiary evidences this debt by a valid Promissory Note payable to me, then such person's portion of my estate shall be diminished by the amount of such debt.

_____ Any and all debts of my estate shall first be paid
__ from my residuary estate. Any debts on any real property bequeathed in this Will shall be assumed by the person to receive such real property and not paid by my Executor.

_____ I direct that my remains be cremated and that the ashes be disposed of according to the wishes of my

__   Executor.

_____   I direct that my remains be cremated and that the
__   ashes be disposed of in the following manner:

_____

_____

_____

_____

_____

_____

_____ I desire to be buried in the
__   _____ cemetery in
_____ County, [State].

IX. SEVERABILITY AND SURVIVAL If any portion of my will shall be held illegal, invalid or otherwise inoperative, it is my intention that all of the other provisions hereof shall continue to be fully effective and operative insofar as is possible and reasonable.

IN WITNESS WHEREOF, I,
_____ [Name of Testator], hereby set my hand to this last Will, on each page of which I have placed my initials, on this _____ day of _____, 20_____ at
_____

___, State of [State].

_____ [Signature]

_____ [Printed or typed
name of Testator]

_____ [Address of
Testator, Line 1]

_____ [Address of
Testator, Line 2]

WITNESSES

The foregoing instrument, consisting of _____ pages,
including this page, was signed in our presence by
_____ [name of Testator]
and declared by _____ [him or her] to be
_____ [his or her] last Will. We, at the request
and in the presence of _____ [him or her] and in
the presence of each other, have subscribed our names
below as witnesses. We declare that we are of sound mind
and of the proper age to witness a will, that to the best of
our knowledge the testator is of the age of majority, or is
otherwise legally competent to make a will, and appears of
sound mind and under no undue influence or constraint.
Under penalty of perjury, we declare these statements are
true and correct on this _____ day of
_____, 20_____ at

_____

___, State of [State].

_____ [Signature of
Witness #1]

_____ [Printed or typed
name of Witness #1]

_____ [Address of Witness
#1, Line 1]
_____ [Address of Witness
#1, Line 2]

_____ [Signature of
Witness #2]
_____ [Printed or typed
name of Witness #2]
_____ [Address of Witness
#2, Line 1]
_____ [Address of Witness
#2, Line 2]

_____ [Signature of
Witness #3]
_____ [Printed or typed
name of Witness #3]
_____ [Address of Witness
#3, Line 1]
_____ [Address of Witness
#3, Line 2]

NOTICE

The information in this document is designed to provide an outline that you can follow when formulating business or personal plans. Due to the variances of many local, city, county and state laws, we recommend that you seek professional legal counseling before entering into any contract or agreement.

Medical Information

MEDICAL HISTORY INFORMATION SHEET
NAME: _____
AGE: _____
Birth Date: (M / D / Year) ____/____/_____
Height ____ft ____inches
Weight _____lbs
Blood Type _____
Hospital Preference:
_____

PAST MEDICAL HISTORY: Please check any
illnesses/conditions which YOU have had.
PTSD___High Blood Pressure___ DVT Lung Disease___
Stroke ___
High Cholesterol___ Pulmonary Embolus___ Asthma___
Diabetes___
Vein Trouble___ Tuberculosis___ Heart Trouble___
Pneumonia___
Kidney Disease___ Nervous Disorder___ Seasonal
Allergies___ HIV___
Thyroid Problems___ Sinus___ Arthritis___ Hepatitis___
Drug Abuse/Alcoholism___ Tonsillitis___
Gastrointestinal___ Osteoporosis___
Joint Replacement___ Bleeding Tendencies___ Cancer:___ If
Yes, What Type_____
Other:
_____

History of Serious Injuries / Illnesses? YES___NO___
 If yes, please describe below.
_____

SURGICAL HISTORY and or SURGICAL COMPLICATIONS?
Please list
_____
_____

FAMILY MEDICAL HISTORY:
Please check any illnesses/conditions immediate FAMILY
has had.
High Blood Pressure___ DVT Lung Disease___ Stroke ___
High Cholesterol___ Pulmonary Embolus___ Asthma___
Diabetes___
Vein Trouble___ Tuberculosis___ Heart Trouble___
Pneumonia___
Kidney Disease___ Nervous Disorder___ Seasonal
Allergies___ HIV___
Liver Disease___ Seizures___ Ear Problems___
Thyroid Problems___ Sinus___ Arthritis___ Hepatitis___
Drug Abuse/Alcoholism___ Tonsillitis___
Gastrointestinal___ Osteoporosis___
Joint Replacement___ Bleeding Tendencies___ Cancer:___ If
Yes, What Type_____

SOCIAL HISTORY:
Occupation: _____
Marital Status: _____
Children: Yes___ No___
Live Alone: Yes___ No___
Tobacco Use: Never___In the Past___ Presently___ How
Much? ___ How Long? ___
Alcohol Use: Daily ___ Occasional ___None ___
Other substance use or abuse? Yes ___ No ___

SYSTEM REVIEW:
Please describe any active problem or symptom.
General Symptoms (i.e. fever, weight gain/loss, fatigue)
_____
Eyes/Ears/Nose/Throat _____
Heart _____
Lung _____
Allergies/Rashes _____
Muscles/Bones/Joints _____
Psychiatric _____
Endocrine (Diabetes/Thyroid) _____
Bleeding/Lymph Nodes _____

165

Nerves _____

Skin and/or Breasts _____

OB/Genital/Urinary _____

Abdomen _____

ALLERGIC TO LATEX: Yes___ No___

ALLERGICTO MEDICATIONS: Yes___ No___

PLEASE LIST:

_____

CURRENT MEDICATIONS:

_____

_____

Misc. Information

List anything that is in your spouse's name or both of your names that you need information on (serial numbers, weapons, passcodes, pin number, hiding places, inventory of work items like truck, boat, etc.) that is not already listed in one of these forms:

_____

_____

_____

_____

_____

_____

_____

_____

_____

_____

_____

_____

_____

_____

_____

_____

_____

_____

_____

_____

_____

_____

_____

_____

Password Keeper

Website:

_____

Website Address:

_____

Username:

_____

Password:

_____

Account Number:

_____

Website:

_____

Website Address:

_____

Username:

_____

Password:

_____

Account Number:

_____

Power of Attorney

I.   NOTICE

This legal document grants you (Hereinafter referred to as the "Principal") the right to transfer unlimited financial powers to someone else (Hereinafter referred to as the "Attorney – in - Fact"), unlimited financial powers are described as: all financial decision making power legal under law. The Principal's transfer of financial powers to the Attorney-in-Fact are granted upon authorization of this agreement, and DO NOT stay in effect in the event of incapacitation by the Principal (incapacitation is described in Paragraph II). This agreement does not authorize the Attorney-in-Fact to make medical
decisions for the Principal. The Principal continues to retain every right to all their financial decision making power and may revoke this General Power of Attorney Form at anytime. The Principal may include restrictions or requests pertaining to the financial decision making power of the Attorney-in-Fact. It is the intent of the Attorney-in-Fact to act in the Principal's wishes put forth, or, to make financial decisions that fit the Principal's best interest. All parties authorizing this agreement must be at least 18 years of age and acting under no false pressures or outside influences. Upon authorization of this General Power of Attorney Form, it will revoke any previously valid General Power of Attorney Form.

II. INCAPACITATION

The powers granted to the Attorney-in-Fact by the Principal in this General Power of Attorney Form DO NOT stay in effect upon incapacitation by the Principal, incapacitation is describes as: A medical physician stating verbally or in writing that the Principal can no longer make decisions for them self.

III. REVOCATION

The Principal has the right to revoke this General Power of Attorney Form at anytime. Any revocation will be effective if the Principal either:
A. Authorizes a new General Power of Attorney Form.
B. Authorizes a Power of Attorney Revocation Form.

IV. WITNESS & NOTARY
This document is not valid as a General Power of Attorney unless it is acknowledged before a notary public or is signed by at least two adult witnesses who are present when the Principal signs or acknowledges the Principal's signature. It is recommended to have this General Power of Attorney Form notarized.

V. PRINCIPAL
I, _____, residing at

_____

City of _____, State of
_____, appoint the following as my Attorney-in-Fact, whom I trust with any and all my financial decision making power immediately upon the authorization of this form:

VI. ATTORNEY-IN-FACT
_____, residing at

_____

City of _____, State of _____
grant the Attorney-in-Fact the legal authority to act on my behalf for any power legal under law in regard to my financial decisions under the State of

_____.

VII. SUCCESSOR ATTORNEY-IN-FACT (Optional)
If the Attorney-in-Fact named above cannot or is unwilling to serve, then I appoint _____, residing at

_____

City of _____, State of _____
grant the Attorney-in-Fact the legal authority to act on my behalf for any power legal under law in regard to my financial decisions under the State of

_____.

VI. TERMS & CONDITIONS
Upon authorization by all parties, the Attorney-in-Fact
accepts their designation to act in the Principal's best
interests for all financial decisions legal under law.

IX. THIRD PARTIES
I, the Principal, agree that any third party receiving a copy
via: physical copy, email, or fax that I, the Principal, will
indemnify and
hold harmless any and all claims that may be put forth in
reference to this Durable Power of Attorney Form.

X. COMPENSATION
The Attorney-in-Fact agrees not to be compensated for
acting in the presence of the Principal. The Attorney-in-Fact
may be, but not
entitled to, reimbursement for all: food, travel, and lodging
expenses for acting in the presence of the Principal.

XI. DISCLOSURE
I intend for my attorney-in-fact under this Power of
Attorney to be treated, as I would be with respect to my
rights regarding the use and
disclosure of my individually identifiable health information
or other medical records. This release authority applies to
any information governed by the Health Insurance
Portability and Accountability Act of 1996 (aka HIPAA), 42
USC 1320d and 45 CFR 160-164

XII. PRINCIPAL'S SIGNATURE
I, _____, thePrincipal, sign my name to
this power of attorney this _____ day of
_____ and, being first duly sworn, do declare
to the undersigned authority that I sign and execute this
instrument as my power of attorney and that I sign it
willingly, or willingly direct another to sign for me, that I
execute it as my free and voluntary act for the purposes
expressed in the
power of attorney and that I am eighteen years of age or
older, of sound mind and under no constraint or undue

influence.

_____

Signature of Principal

XIII. ATTORNEY-IN-FACT'S SIGNATURE

I, _____ have read the attached power of attorney and am the person identified as the attorney-in-fact for the principal. I hereby acknowledge and accept my appointment as Attorney-in-Fact and that when I act as agent I shall exercise

the powers for the benefit of the principal; I shall keep the assets of the principal separate from my assets; I shall exercise reasonable caution and prudence; and I shall keep a full and accurate record

of all actions, receipts and disbursements on behalf of the principal.

_____

Signature of Attorney-In-Fact

XIV. Notary Acknowledgement

(Must be completed by Notary)

State of _____ County of _____

_____ Subscribed, Sworn and acknowledged before me

by _____, the Principal, and

subscribed and sworn to before me by

_____, witness, this _____

day of _____.

_____

Notary Signature

Notary Public In and for the County of

_____

State of _____

My commission expires: _____

Seal

Acknowledgement and Acceptance of Appointment as Attorney-in-Fact

I, _____ have read the attached power of attorney and am the person identified as the attorney-in-fact for the principal. I hereby acknowledge that

accept my appointment as Attorney-in-Fact and that when I
act as agent I shall exercise the powers for the benefit of the
principal; I shall keep the assets of the principal separate
from my assets; I shall exercise reasonable caution and
prudence; and I shall keep a full and accurate of all actions,
receipts and disbursements on behalf of the principal.

_____

Signature of Attorney-in-Fact

_____

Date

Acceptance of Appointment as successor Attorney-in-Fact
I, _____ have read the attached
power of attorney and am the person identified as the
successor attorney-in-fact for the principal. I hereby
acknowledge that I accept
my appointment as Successor Attorney-in-Fact and that, in
the absence of a specific provision to the contrary in the
power of attorney, when I act as agent I shall exercise the
powers for the benefit of the principal; I shall keep the
assets of the principal separate from my assets; I shall
exercise reasonable caution and prudence; and I shall keep
a full and accurate record of all actions, receipts, and
disbursements on behalf of the principal.

_____

Signature of Successor Attorney-in-Fact

_____

Date
Witness Attestation
I, _____, the first witness, and I

_____

the second witness, sign my name to the foregoing power of
attorney being first duly sworn and do not declare to the
undersigned authority that the principal signs and
executed this instrument as him or her, and that I, in the

presence and hearing of the principal, sign this power of attorney as witness to the principal's signing and that to the best of my knowledge the principal is eighteen years of age or older, of sound mind and under no constraint or undue influence.

_____

Signature of First Witness

_____

Signature of Second Witness

Trust

REVOCABLE LIVING TRUST

I, _____ ,hereby transfer to _____ "Trustee", the property set forth on Schedule A attached hereto and made a part hereof, to be held IN TRUST, for the purposes and in accordance with the provisions which follow:

ARTICLE I: Lifetime Benefits

Prior to my death, my Trustee shall:

(1) pay over to me such part or all of the income or principal of this trust as I may from time to time direct;

(2) pay or apply such part or all of the income and principal of this trust as it may deem necessary to provide for the proper support and maintenance of myself, my wife and my minor children and to provide for any medical or other expenses that I, my wife or my minor children may incur and

ARTICLE II: Coordination with Probate Estate

Following my death, my Trustee shall collect all property distributable to my Trustee as a result of my death whether by will or otherwise. In the collection of proceeds payable under any life insurance policies, payment to and receipt by the Trustee shall be a full discharge of the liability of any insurance company, and any such company need not take notice of this agreement or see to the application of any such payment by the

Trustee. All such property, together with all other property constituting this trust (hereinafter referred to as the trust fund), shall be held, managed and distributed as follows:

If my probate estate (excluding the income thereof) has insufficient liquid assets to pay my funeral expenses, claims against my estate, expenses of administering my estate, death taxes chargeable to my estate and to satisfy all pre-residuary devises under my will, my Trustee shall make available to my Executor, from the trust fund, such sum or sums as my Executor in its sole discretion shall determine to be necessary to satisfy such deficiency; provided my Trustee shall not pay to or otherwise make available for the benefit of my estate or my Executor life insurance proceeds, or any other assets, which would otherwise be exempt from the claims of creditors.

My Trustee shall pay out of principal those expenses connected with the administration of the trust fund (including but not limited to the attorney's fees and Trustee's commissions) incurred after my death.

ARTICLE III

SECTION 1: Allocation of Property to Trust

On the death of Grantor, the trustee shall retain in Trust, the maximum amount of property which Grantor could retain without payment of federal estate taxes giving effect to the maximum unified credit available to Grantor as of the date of Grantor's death. In allocating property to be retained, the trustee shall give first consideration to any property which would not qualify for the Estate Tax Marital Deduction.

In addition to the property allocated above the trustee shall retain any property which remains and which does not qualify for allocation to the Marital Deduction. If, on the death of Grantor, Grantor is not survived by a spouse then all of Grantor's property shall be retained.

Any residue of property not retained as hereinabove provided shall be distributed to Grantor's spouse upon the death of the Grantor.

SECTION 2: Disposition of Income and Principal

After the death of the Grantor, the Trust shall be held and disposed of, as follows:

Payment of Income to Spouse. Commencing with the death of the Grantor, the trustee shall pay the net income at least quarterly to Grantor's surviving spouse for so long as the spouse survives.

Payment of Principal to Spouse. The trustee shall pay to Grantor's surviving spouse so much of the principal, as the trustee, in the trustees sole discretion, from time-to-time believes desirable for the spouses reasonable support, medical care, and education, taking into account, however, other resources available to the spouse which are known to the trustee; PROVIDED, HOWEVER, that no funds or property shall be expended by the trustee under this provision to provide for any goods or services the means for acquisition of which are available from other sources, including, but not limited to, insurance or governmental benefits. Should two or more persons, whether individual or corporate, serve as trustee, and Grantor's spouse serve as one of those trustees, the decision to pay principal to Grantor's spouse shall be made by the trustee or trustees other than Grantor's spouse, and without Grantor's spouse taking part in that decision.

Surviving Children. The trustee shall pay so much or all of the net income and principal of this trust, even to its exhaustion, to each child under age 21 (the termination age) as required, in the judgment of the trustee to (1) provide proper care and support, including housing, food, clothing, and medical and dental expenses; (2) provide an education, including tuition, books, fees, housing, board, spending money, travel, camp and including public or private school, college, university, graduate, professional, or technical school, during such time as the child shall pursue his or her education in good faith; (3) provide funds for a wedding and other necessary social expenses; (4) meet extraordinary or emergency expenses which arise through illness or other misfortune; (5) pay expenses arising out of last illness and burial; or (6) provide for the general welfare and well being. In making income and principal distributions, the trustee may, but is not required to, consider any other income or property available to a child from any other source (including any self-help ability) known to the trustee. Net income not distributed shall be accumulated and become part of the principal. The trustee shall govern aid and assistance to a child with due regard to the future financial requirements of Grantor's other children under the termination age, and for their support, care, and completion of their education. It is Grantor's intent that Grantor's children have equal opportunity but not that the trustee necessarily expend equal dollar amounts on behalf of each child. A child's right to net income and principal, as provided above, terminates when the child attains the termination age, PROVIDED, HOWEVER, that the trustee may pay so much or all of the net income and principal of this trust, even to its exhaustion, as required in the judgment of the trustee, to (a) meet extraordinary or emergency expenses which arise through illness or other misfortune of a child who has already attained the termination age, or (b) provide a child with an education even though the child has already attained the termination age if the trustee shall determine the child has been unavoidably prevented (e.g., military draft, illness, or similar reason) from taking advantage of education opportunities available to children under the termination age. Any child who shall receive any net income or principal under this provision shall not be required to repay the same to this trust nor shall any such payment be set off against the distributive share of the child. Loans to Children. The trustee may also make loans to any child for any of the six (6) purposes specified above or for such purposes as purchasing a home, starting a business, or other similar purposes at any time, regardless of his or her age, provided all such loans shall be made with due regard to the future financial requirements of Grantor's other children under the termination age for their support, care, and completion of their education. All loans shall be repaid as the trustee shall determine and may be secured or unsecured and with or without interest. Family Home. In the event that the family home of Grantor's children shall become an asset of this trust, the family home may be retained for the benefit of all, some, or one of Grantor's children at the expense of the trust. In addition, the trustee may provide financial assistance by outright grant (without obligation for repayment), investment, loan, or otherwise, to the guardian or any other person having the care and custody of Grantor's children for the purpose of providing funds for the purchase, expansion, alteration, or rental of living accommodations for such children, it being Grantor's intent to protect the guardian or any other person having the care and custody of Grantor's children from any significant economic burden by reason of their appointment and to give the trustee broad discretion in assisting the guardian or any other person having the care and custody of Grantor's children in providing living accommodations for Grantor's children. Distribution to Children. When the last of Grantor's children attains the termination age, or if all Grantor's children have attained the termination age at Grantor's death, the trustee shall divide and distribute all principal and undistributed net income of this trust into equal shares, one for each child surviving, and one for each child, not surviving but leaving a child of his or her own, share and share alike, per stripes and not per capita.

SECTION 3: Death of Child

If any child dies before complete distribution of that child's separate share and leaves no descendants surviving, that child's share shall be divided into equal shares for Grantor's remaining children and be continued in trust or distributed as provided in this trust.

SECTION 4: Residuary Distribution

If, at any time following the creation of this trust, Grantor and Grantor's spouse and issue should all die without having acquired the rights to the immediate payment of all the property held in trust for them, the trustee shall terminate this trust and pay all property held by the trustee to my heirs at law.

ARTICLE IV: Revocability

I reserve the right to amend or revoke this agreement, without the consent of any other person, by a writing signed by me and delivered to my Trustee; provided that the duties, responsibilities and compensation of my Trustee shall not be altered without my Trustee's written consent.

ARTICLE V: Fiduciary Powers

I grant my Trustee and any successor Trustee the authority and power to exercise, in its sole discretion and without court order, in respect of any property forming part of any trust created under this agreement or otherwise in its possession hereunder, all powers conferred by law upon trustees, or expressed in this agreement, and I intend that the powers so granted be construed in the broadest possible manner. In addition, my Trustee shall also have the power, authority and discretion hereinafter set forth:

(1) Facility of Payments: To apply for the benefit of, or to the use of, any person, any property, whether principal or income vesting in or payable to such person, without seeing to the application of the payments so made and for which the receipt of the payee shall fully discharge my Trustee from obligation.

(2) Non-Pro Rata Distribution: To make distributions under this agreement (without the consent of any beneficiary) in cash or in specific property, real or personal, or in undivided interests therein, or partly in cash and partly in such property, and to do so without regard to the income tax basis of specific property allocated to any beneficiary (including any trust) and without making pro rata divisions of specific assets.

(3) Holdback Trusts: To withhold distribution of any property, whether principal or income, vesting pursuant to the provisions of this agreement in any person who is then under twenty-one (21) years of age and, if this power is exercised, the continuing power to hold such property in trust for such person; to apply such part of the income or principal therefrom at such times and in such amounts as my Trustee shall deem requisite or desirable for the support and education of such person; and to accumulate and add to trust principal all current income not so applied until such person attains twenty-one (21) years of age, or shall sooner die, whereupon the property then remaining in the trust shall be distributed to such person or to the personal representative of such person's estate, as the case may be.

(4) Elimination of Small Trusts: To terminate or not establish any trust created or to be created under this agreement (other than a qualified charitable remainder trust) whenever the total fair market value of the assets of any such trust is so small that my Trustee's annual fee for administering the trust would be the minimum annual fee set forth in my Trustee's regularly published fee schedule then in effect, or whenever my Trustee determines it would be contrary to the best interest of the beneficiaries by

reason of legislation or unforeseen changes or circumstances to create or continue such a trust, in which event the property then constituting or receivable by such trust shall be distributed to the beneficiaries then entitled to the income of such trust. If the beneficiaries of such income depend upon the exercise of my Trustee's discretion, then my Trustee shall distribute such property among those beneficiaries and in such proportions as my Trustee, in its sole discretion, shall determine, and its determination shall be binding and conclusive upon all interested persons.

(5) Transactions Between Related Entities: To sell assets of any trust created under this agreement to itself, as Executor or Trustee of any other trust or estate, to the beneficiaries thereof or to any member of my family at the fair market value thereof, and to purchase assets from any other such trust or estate, or from the beneficiaries thereof, or from any member of my family for any trust created under this agreement at the fair market value thereof; and, to the extent allowed by law, to lend money to itself as Executor or Trustee of such other trusts or estates, or to the beneficiaries thereof, or to any member of my family at rates of interest and with security determined by my Trustee to be adequate; providing I, my spouse, my parents or my descendants are the respective grantor's or decedents of such other trusts or estates.

(6) Court Accounting and Bond Excused: My Trustee shall not be required to qualify, to make or file any inventory, appraisal, account or report to any court or to give bond (unless in each instance it is otherwise required to do so notwithstanding this provision), but shall be required to furnish at least annually to each current beneficiary a statement giving a summary of receipts and disbursements during each accounting period and assets on hand at the end of the accounting period. Such accountings are deemed correct and are accepted if no notice to the contrary is received within 90 days.

(7) Merger of Trusts: To merge the assets of any trust created under this agreement (other than a trust qualifying for the marital deduction) with those of any other trust, by whomsoever created, maintained for the same beneficiaries upon substantially the same terms (even though the component trusts differ as to contingent beneficiaries, in which case, if the contingency occurs, the funds may be distributed in such shares as my Trustee, in its sole discretion, deems necessary to create a fair ratio between the various sets of remainder men); provided, however, that property which would otherwise remain exempt from generation-skipping taxes shall not be merged with any other trust.

(8) Retention of Trustee's Stock: To retain any shares of stock which I may own at the time of my death in my Trustee or in the bank holding company of which my Trustee is a subsidiary or any affiliate company, or in any successor corporation to my Trustee or holding company; to exercise rights to purchase its own stock or securities convertible into its own stock when offered pro rata to stockholders and to purchase additional fractional shares to round out fractional share holdings of its stock occasioned by such exercises or by the receipt of a stock dividend.

(9) Withholding For Taxes: To withhold distribution of an amount of property sufficient, in its judgment, to cover any liability that may be imposed on my Trustee for estate or other taxes until such liability is finally determined and paid.

(10) Investment of Cash: To invest and reinvest any income or proceeds from trust assets in short-term investment funds or accounts pending instructions from me as to the disposition or investment thereof.

(11) Provisions Regarding Holding and Management of Real Property:

(a) To deal with matters involving the actual or threatened contamination of trust property (including interests in sole proprietorships, partnerships or corporations and any assets owned by such business entities) by hazardous substances, or involving compliance with environmental laws. In particular, my Trustee is empowered:

(i) To inspect any such property periodically, as it deems necessary, to determine compliance with any environmental law affecting such property, with all expenses of such inspection and monitoring to be paid from the income or principal of the trust;

(ii) To respond (or take any other action necessary to prevent, abate or clean up) as it shall deem necessary, prior to or after the initiation of enforcement action by any governmental body, to any actual or threatened violation of any environmental law affecting any of such property, the cost of which shall be payable from trust assets;

(iii) To refuse to accept property as a trust asset if it determines that such property is contaminated by any hazardous substance or that such property is being used or has been used for any activities directly or indirectly involving hazardous substances which could result in liability to the trust or otherwise impair the value of trust assets;

(iv) To settle or compromise at any time any claim against this trust related to any such matter asserted by any governmental body or private party;

(v) To disclaim any power which it determines may cause it to incur personal liability as a result of such matters, whether such power is set forth in this document, incorporated by reference herein, or granted or implied by any statute or rule of law;

(vi) To decline to serve as Trustee or, having undertaken to serve, resign at any time it believes there is or may be a conflict between it in its fiduciary capacity and in its

individual capacity because of potential claims or liabilities
which might be asserted against this trust because of the
type or condition of trust assets.

(b) My Trustee shall not be personally liable to any
beneficiary or other party interested in this trust, or to any
third parties, for any claim against the trust for the
diminution in value of trust property resulting from such
matters, including any reporting of or response to (1) the
contamination of trust property by hazardous substances,
or (2) violations of environmental laws related to my trust;
provided that my Trustee shall not be excused from liability
for its own negligence or wrongful or willful acts;

(c) When used in this document the term hazardous
substance shall mean any substance defined as hazardous
or toxic or otherwise regulated by any federal, state or local
law, rule or regulation relating to the protection of the
environment or human health (environmental law);

(d) On behalf of myself and my successors, heirs and
assigns, I hereby indemnify and hold harmless my Trustee
from and against any and all claims, liabilities, penalties
and costs, including attorneys' fees, arising from any claim,
demand, order or other action related in any way to (1) the
actual or threatened contamination of trust property by any
hazardous substance, or (2) the generation, use, treatment,
storage, disposal, release (actual or threatened) or
discharge on or from trust property or in connection with
operations conducted on trust property of any hazardous
substance in violation of any environmental law.

(12) Renounce Powers: Following my death, to renounce, in
whole or in part, any rights, privileges, powers and
immunities granted to my Trustee, whether such rights,
privileges, powers and immunities are granted under this
agreement or conferred by law, by executing and filing a
written renunciation with the clerk of court of the county in
which proceedings have been commenced for the
administration of my estate. My Trustee's assumption of

duties as fiduciary shall not waive or bar my Trustee's right to renounce any right, privilege, power or immunity.

(13) Income and Principal Apportionment: The Trustee shall have discretion to determine whether items should be charged or credited to income or principal, or be apportioned between income and principal, including the power to provide or not to provide a reasonable reserve against depreciation, depletion or obsolescence. The Trustee shall exercise its discretion in such manner as it may reasonably deem equitable and just under all the circumstances and regardless of whether such items are charged or credited to or apportioned between income and principal as provided in _____ Statutes.

Notwithstanding any other provision of this agreement to the contrary, no power or authority conferred by law or expressed or specifically incorporated in this agreement shall be exercised in a manner which would cause any distribution hereunder for the benefit of my spouse which would otherwise qualify for the federal estate tax marital deduction to fail to qualify for such deduction. My spouse shall have the power to require my Trustee to make productive any non-income producing property in any trust which would otherwise qualify for the federal estate tax marital deduction, or to convert such property into productive property within a reasonable period of time.

ARTICLE VI: Resignation

My Trustee or any successor Trustee may resign during my lifetime by giving me thirty (30) days notice in writing, whereupon I shall have the right to appoint a successor Trustee. Delivery to the successor Trustee or to me, if I do not appoint a successor Trustee, and proper accounting for all property received and disbursed by my Trustee shall discharge my Trustee from all responsibility and liability with respect to and in connection with this trust.

After my death my Trustee, or any successor Trustee, may resign as Trustee of any trust being held under this agreement in a writing signed and acknowledged and delivered to all current adult income beneficiaries of such trust, such resignation to be effective upon a successor Trustee being appointed to act in its place. No judicial proceeding shall be necessary. A majority of the beneficiaries entitled to receive such notice shall have the power to sign an acknowledged writing delivered to the then acting Trustee appointing a successor Trustee.

Any successor corporate Trustee domiciled outside the State of _____ and duly appointed hereunder, shall be authorized to remove any personal property constituting the principal of such trust to the domicile of the successor corporate Trustee; provided that the laws in the State of _____ shall continue to govern the rights of beneficiaries in such property and the manner in which such trust is construed and administered.

Any successor Trustee is authorized and directed to accept from any prior Trustee the assets delivered by such predecessor on the basis of the predecessor's accounting for such assets without requiring an audit or other independent accounting of the transactions, acts or omissions of such prior Trustee, and any successor Trustee shall not have any duty, responsibility, obligation or liability whatsoever for the acts or omissions of such prior Trustee.

ARTICLE VII: Situs

This agreement shall be construed and the trusts created by this agreement shall be regulated and governed in accordance with the laws of the State of _____.

ARTICLE VIII: Compensation of Fiduciary

As compensation for its services hereunder, my Trustee shall receive the commissions stipulated in its regularly adopted schedule of compensation in effect and applicable at the time of the performance of such services.

ACCEPTANCE CLAUSE

In Witness Whereof, I do hereby sign and seal this instrument, and my Trustee in executing same hereby acknowledges receipt of property set forth on Schedule A and accepts the trust created hereunder and covenants to faithfully discharge all duties of its office as Trustee, this _____ day of _____ (month), _____ (year).

_____

Name of Grantor

_____

Trustee

CWHQ Contact Inforamtion

Cop Wives Headquarters:

admins@mycwhq.com

Please contact any of the above with questions or if you are in a situation and need our assistance.

Made in the USA
Middletown, DE
13 March 2018